EDUCATIONAL IMPLICATIONS OF SELF-CONCEPT THEORY

WALLACE D. LABENNE

BERT I. GREENE

Eastern Michigan University

GOODYEAR PUBLISHING COMPANY, INC.
Pacific Palisades, California

0876202474

Library of Congress Catalog Card Number: 71-92020

Current printing (last digit):
10 9 8 7 6

Printed in the United States of America

PREFACE

During the last decade, self-concept theory as a meaningful psychological construct explaining the why of human behavior has had a resurgence in the field of education. It is somewhat gratifying to observe the emphasis that schools and in-service education programs place on the self-concept theory. There is little doubt that educators are becoming more concerned with what happens to their students' personalities as well as their mental faculties. In such a setting the focus of this book is the scrutiny of current educational practices in terms of whether they enhance or destroy the self status of students.

We were not content with a mere presentation of developmental progression, motivation for growth, or the perceptual process of learning as fundamental psychological principles. These points are certainly important to educators; but it is not enough simply to know them. The educator must indeed become a practitioner involved in the implementation of sound theory. After all, it is the teacher who comes into daily contact with students and must necessarily influence them. This direct contact and subtle transmission of attitudes and values is our main concern here.

Our viewpoint is that teachers have no right to constantly ignore policies, curricular practices, teaching methodology, and classroom experiences that are potentially dangerous to their students. Teachers cannot turn aside from these matters and feel that their only task is to teach a subject and maintain control of the classroom. Society's most precious possession has been entrusted to teachers, and they are obligated not to betray that trust and confidence. It seems, then, that we have plunged into the arena of controversy concerning current educational practices and have taken a decided position in keeping with the stark reality of self-concept theory.

Empirical and experimental data demonstrate a direct relationship between the child's self-concept and his manifest behavior, perceptions, and academic performance. Where specific evidence is lacking, we have carefully weighed the merits and consequences of teaching activities in terms of their probable influence on the child's developing self-conception. In this manner, we have discussed the issues and maintained consistency with the theory. It must, of course, be recognized that every theory loses something in the translation into practice. We have tried to minimize that deficiency.

While we are aware of the many influences peripheral to the school which impinge upon the child's self, we maintain that the school is a major contributing agent to the malleable status of the child's conception of self. Furthermore, we recognize our limitations in reaching parents and other significant adults. We do not claim that the school alone can do the job; in fact, the opposite is true. We cannot deny, however, the importance of the school and school personnel and the impact of these on a child's life. While teachers cannot control the student's total environment, the few hours each child is in school are the direct responsibility of the teacher. These hours form the central focus of this work.

The chapters in this book fall into three basic categories: orientation, application, and determination. The first category comprises the first three chapters. Here a perspective on the origin of self-concept theory, an elucidation of the theory as an operationally useful construct to teachers, and an overview of the educational implications are presented. The second category, application, comprises the succeeding five chapters. Questions that in practice arise concerning the use of intelligence tests, ability grouping, grading, promotion, and classroom discipline are answered in terms of self-concept theory. Finally, the third category looks at how the self-concept is measured and at some of the difficulties involved in that measurement.

We sincerely hope that both student and veteran teachers alike will examine the policies and practices of their present persuasion in the light of whether they negate or support the theoretical premise emphasized in this work. It is our further desire that undergraduate and graduate courses that address themselves to human development, mental hygiene, psychological foundations of education, and teaching principles will expose students to the considerations presented in this book.

W. D. LaB.

Ypsilanti, Michigan   B. I. G.

ACKNOWLEDGMENTS

In addition to quotations specifically cited, the authors wish to thank the following for permission to reprint materials included in this book:

The Pointer: for Special Class Teachers and Parents of the Handicapped—for selection from "Grading: Discriminating or Disintegrating" by Wallace D. La Benne, Spring, 1968.

Psychology: A Journal of Human Behavior—for selection from "A Theoretical Framework for Behavior Analysis and Intervention" by Wallace D. La Benne, May, 1968.

Psychology: A Journal of Human Behavior—for selection from "Self-Concept: Educational Implications" by Wallace D. La Benne, August, 1968.

CONTENTS

Chapter 7

GRADING PRACTICES   76

Chapter 8

CLASSROOM DISCIPLINE   91

Chapter 9

THE MEASUREMENT OF SELF-CONCEPT   109

Chapter **10**

SUPPLEMENTARY CONSIDERATIONS   120

Chapter **1**

HISTORICAL
PERSPECTIVE

Self-concept as a determinant of human behavior is not a recent theoretical formulation. The Hindu scriptures, in the first century B.C., state:

> Oh, let the self exalt itself,
> Not sink itself below;
> Self is the only friend of self,
> And self self's only foe.

> For self, when it subdues itself
> Befriends itself. And so
> When it eludes self-conquest, is
> Its own and only foe.

> So calm, so self-subdued, the self
> Has an unshaken base
> Through pain and pleasure, cold and heat
> Through honor and disgrace.

1

From the earliest recorded history of man there is evidence that he has sought to understand the causes of his conduct. An awareness of this quest and curiosity is found primarily in the context of religious thought. The most primitive religions consider man to have some inner regulatory agent which influences his destiny or responds to a supernatural force. This "inner agent" has been variously labeled "soul," "flesh," "nature," "breath," "will," and other such names. Today, scientific "self-psychology" rejects these metaphysical conjectures of a psychic agent; it rather considers *self-concept* as a hypothetical construct inferred from behavior. Perceptual psychology now accepts the idea that the feelings and beliefs one holds about oneself motivate one's conduct: the antecedent for individual responses is the self-concept.

James

Since 1860, when psychology became an official discipline and science of human behavior, self-concept has had cyclic resurgence and fallowness. It would be proper to say that much of the contemporary theorizing about self-concept derives from William James.[1] He considered ego the individual's sense of identity. In addition to this global concept, he felt that self included spiritual, material, and social aspects. Mental faculties and inclinations comprised the spiritual self. Material possessions constituted the material self. The esteem and regard that a person perceives others have for him formed the social self. James also gave the self a dynamic quality in terms of self-preservation and seeking. From James, then, came a view of self which incorporated feelings and attitudes along with a principle of causality.

About a half century after James' writings, a number of theorists began to establish and elucidate their concepts of self. Although each of these theorists introduced his preferred jargon, all used the term "self" to have one of three meanings: (1) a dynamic process; (2) a system of awareness; or (3) an interrelated process and awareness. The first meaning incorporated the cognition processes, such as perceiving, interpreting, thinking, and remembering. The second denoted the objectified form of awareness an individual gives to his feelings, evaluations, and beliefs about himself. The third gave the body of awareness a psychodynamic quality in terms of its effect

[1] William James, *Principles of Psychology*, 2 vols. (New York: Holt, Rinehart and Winston, Inc., 1890).

upon what is perceived, of how this perception is interpreted, and thus of human behavior and learning.

Allport

Allport,[2] like James, articulated on the interrelatedness of the self as both object and process with a measure of clarity. He was especially cautious about the use of the term "self" in order to avoid the factotum or agent theories of prescientific psychology. Yet, his contributions to an operationally useful concept of a dynamic self have been considerable. Allport calls the ego, or self, functions the propriate functions of the personality. The "proprium" comprises awareness of self and striving activity; it includes bodily sense, self-image, self-esteem, and identity as well as thinking and knowing. The proprium of personality gives stability and consistency to evaluations, intentions, and attitudes. For Allport, the terms self and ego should be used as descriptive adjectives to indicate the propriate functions of the personality.

Freud

Although Freud's writings were concurrent with the beginning period of scientific psychology, much of his theory is mythological and empirically untestable. Much of the dynamics of his theory finds its basis in prescientific instinct postulations. Nevertheless, Freud [3] gives the ego a central place in his theory of personality structure. In counterdistinction to James and Allport, Freud pays little attention to the self-image. Rather, for him the ego is a functional agent or executive of the personality which makes rational choices and controls action in the healthy person. The ego decides what instincts to satisfy as well as in what manner to satisfy them. It prevents the discharge of tension until the appropriate time. The ego keeps a "psychic balance" between the demands of the moral arm of the personality and the natural impulses of the person. To the extent that the ego is able to keep harmony between the impulses and conscience, it is an effective agent.

2 G. W. Allport, *Personality: A Psychological Interpretation* (New York: Holt, Rinehart and Winston, Inc., 1937).

3 S. Freud, *A General Introduction to Psychoanalysis* (Garden City, New York: Garden City Publishing Co., 1943).

Mead

In contrast to Freud's conception of the ego as a system of processes is Mead's self as an object of awareness. Mead [4] claims that the person responds to himself with certain feelings and attitudes as others respond to him. He becomes self-conscious (aware) by the way people react to him as an object. Further, various selves can be differentiated by the specific set of responses in different social settings. Home attitudes expressed toward him create a home self; school attitudes expressed by teachers and classroom experiences create a school self; and social attitudes expressed by peers and others in social settings create a social self.

Of the number of theorists briefly reviewed in this chapter, Freud and Mead most clearly represent the segregated meanings of self as process and as object, respectively. James and Allport point the direction which we here find as a plausible dynamic theory of personality. We will review Combs and Snygg in terms of the theory adopted for this work at the conclusion of the present chapter. Prior to these considerations, we will note other theories for their subtle additions to an understanding of self-concept.

Lewin

According to Lewin, [5] the self-concept is represented by a life space region which determines present belief about the self. The term "life space" is a psychological concept to be distinguished from physical space. It includes the individual's universe of personal experience as a space in which he moves. Goals, evaluations, ideas, perceptions of significant objects, future plans and events, all form a part of the life space of the person. Life space can be considered a complex internal mechanism which produces behavior. All the variables that determine the direction of behavior lie in the life space of the individual. If one is to predict behavior, one must know the life space of the person at the time the behavior is to be predicted. By the same token, if one desires to change behavior, one must alter the valences of the subject's life space. Lewin's life space

[4] G. H. Mead, *Mind, Self, and Society* (Chicago: University of Chicago Press, 1934).

[5] K. Lewin, *Principles of Topological Psychology* (New York: McGraw-Hill Book Company, 1936).

closely parallels the meaning of an objectified form of self. But Lewin gives Mead's self a functional process of causality that is dynamically active through a mechanism which he chooses to call "life space."

Lundholm

Lundholm,[6] another self-psychologist, distinguishes between a subjective self and an objective self. No mention of the functional, motivational, or process dynamics of the self is explicitly stated. The subjective self is mainly what a person comes to think about himself. Lundholm views the subjective self as alterable from the experiences one has in interaction with others in the pursuit of various tasks. This theory is similar to Mead's, in that the self is primarily an object of awareness.

Sherif and Cantril

Sherif and Cantril[7] vaguely assert that the self is an object and the ego is a process. They conceive of the ego as a constellation of attitudes that include personal identity, values, possessions, and feelings of worth. Although they do not clearly differentiate self as object and ego as process, they do imply that when the ego becomes involved in a given task it will energize and direct the person's behavior. For instance, if self-esteem is at stake, the ego attitudes are aroused and tend to motivate the person to work much harder.

Symonds

Symonds[8] incorporates the psychoanalytic theory of Freud and the social philosophy of Mead and thus sees the ego as a group of processes and the self as the manner in which the individual reacts to himself. While ego and self are distinct aspects of personality, there is considerable interaction between them. There is a favorable

[6] Helge Lundholm, "Reflections Upon the Nature of the Psychological Self," *Psychological Review,* 47 (1940), 110–27.

[7] M. Sherif and H. Cantril, *The Psychology of Ego-Involvement* (New York: John Wiley & Sons, Inc., 1947).

[8] P. M. Symonds, *The Ego and The Self* (New York: Appleton-Century-Crofts, 1951).

self-reaction when the ego performs effectively in meeting the demands of life. On the other hand, the ego functions more effectively when the self is confident and held in high regard. Symonds cautions that a person may be unaware of his true self-conceptions due to unconscious distortions. In other words, what a person says about himself may not necessarily agree with his unconscious self-evaluations.[9]

Cattell

Cattell considers "the self" the principal organizing influence exerted upon man which gives stability and order to human behavior. He differentiates between the concept of self (awareness) and sentiment of self. The sentiment of self-regard is the most important influence in man. Cattell states that sentiments are the ". . . major acquired dynamic trait structures which cause their possessors to pay attention to certain objects, or class of objects, and to feel and react in a certain way with regard to them." [10] Here we have selective perception as it relates to self-concept.

Cattell also introduces the process of self-observation. The self which a person must rationally admit to be is the actual (real) self, and the self which a person would aspire to is the ideal self. Cattell, along with James, Allport, and Lewin, conceives of the self as both object and process. While James gives the self a dynamic quality of self-preservation and seeking, and Allport gives it the "propriate" function of striving activity, Cattell is even more explicit in terms of selective perception and maintenance of self-esteem, and adds the dimension of aspirational self.

Murphy

Where Cattell expands the self-functions, Murphy [11] expands objectified self, as does Mead, and delimits the self-process primarily to defensive-enhancing functions. Murphy presents a number of selves dynamically interconnected in the form of a total organiza-

---

[9] The discrepancies between self-reports and self-concepts are examined in Chapters 2 and 9.

[10] R. B. Cattell, *Personality: A Systematic, Theoretical, and Factual Study* (New York: McGraw-Hill Book Company, 1950), p. 161.

[11] G. Murphy, *Personality: A Biosocial Approach to Origins and Structures* (New York: Harper & Row, Publishers, 1947).

tion. He defines "self" as the individual as known to the individual. This derives from a person's conceptions and perceptions of his total being, including such selves as the frustrated self and the ideal self. Murphy attributes the defensive mechanisms to the ego processes. The major activities of the ego are to defend and/or enhance the self complex.

Rogers

Unlike Symonds who cautions that a person's unconscious self-evaluations may distort his self-concept, Rogers believes in the discontinuity of the unconscious and conscious. We believe that this discontinuity is of major significance in order to understand self-concept theory. People behave in terms of the ways in which they see themselves—a conscious activity. Rogers allows for the probability of an unconscious reservoir, but implies that only when information about self and the environment is "admissible to awareness" does it influence behavior. He states: "As long as the self-Gestalt is firmly organized, and no contradictory material is even dimly perceived, then positive self-feelings may exist, the self may be seen as worthy and acceptable, and conscious tension is minimal. Behavior is consistent with the organized hypotheses and concepts of the self-structure." [12] The consistency between behavior and self-concepts indicates the dual role of self: self as object and self as process.

Snygg and Combs

Snygg and Combs are the clearest representatives of the self-concept theory to which we subscribe. Because of the central role they accord to conscious feelings, cognitions, and perceptions, Snygg and Combs are "phenomenologists." They claim that "all behavior, without exception, is completely determined by and pertinent to the phenomenal field of the behaving organism." [13] That is, how a person behaves is the result of how he perceives the situation and himself at the moment of his action. In fact, awareness is the cause of behavior: how a person feels and thinks determines his course of

[12] C. R. Rogers, *Client-Centered Therapy: Its Current Practice, Implications and Theory* (Boston: Houghton Mifflin Company, 1951), p. 191.

[13] D. Snygg and A. W. Combs, *Individual Behavior* (New York: Harper & Row, Publishers, 1949), p. 15.

action. Phenomenology, then, is the study of direct awareness. Snygg and Combs give us a phenomenal self which is both an object and a process, thus avoiding arbitrary distinctions and semantic difficulties. Later, Combs succinctly states: "The self is composed of perceptions concerning the individual and this organization of perceptions in turn has vital and important effects upon the behavior of the individual." [14]

There are many other psychologists who have written on self-referent constructs. Those which we selected for discussion are representative of the significant trends leading to the theoretical framework accepted for this work.

Summary

In this chapter, man's search for an understanding of the causes of his conduct has been traced. During the years preceding the establishment of psychology as a science, much of this quest and curiosity was found in the context of religious thought. The development of psychology as a discipline and science of human behavior, however, brought about the rejection of metaphysical conjectures and the establishment of hypothetical constructs. The self-concept, as one such construct, has had many adherents during that time.

Beginning with James (in 1890), who viewed self as incorporating feelings and attitudes and a dynamic quality in terms of self-preservation and seeking, one finds many noted psychologists contributing to the field of self-referent constructs. The differences and similarities in the theories of James, Allport, Freud, Lewin, Rogers, and others are examined in order to understand the role of the self-concept.

All these theorists have made valuable contributions to self-concept theory. We feel, however, that Snygg and Combs are the clearest representatives of the theory to which we ourselves subscribe. The self, as it is viewed in this work, is presented as both object and process, and the individual is seen to behave according to how he perceives the situation and himself at the moment of his action.

[14] A. W. Combs, "Snygg and Combs' Phenomenal Self," *Theories of Personality,* Hall and Lindzey, eds. (New York: John Wiley & Sons, Inc., 1963), p. 470.

Chapter 2

DEVELOPMENT AND DYNAMICS OF SELF-CONCEPT

The term "self-concept" is so widely used in education today that one assumes that this term is generally understood. This means that the definition as given is accepted, if for no other reason than for the purpose of communication. Self-concept is a psychological *construct,* however, or an imaginary mechanism which helps the psychologist think about the phenomena he is studying. It is virtually impossible to discuss behavior in terms of modern psychological theory without resorting to constructs. A construct, however, is not an inner entity, a specific substance, or a psychic agent which can be seen or measured directly. Instead, it is a concept of self inferred from behavior.

Constructs—a Linking Mechanism

The danger involved herein is that a construct, which is postulated from events that are inferred indirectly, as opposed to observable events, is sometimes treated as if it were a real, observable event when it gains broad usage. This process is known as reification, or the making real of something that is not real. When this happens, people begin to speak about a construct as if it were real, and sometimes they define it in terms of behavior. This process is in direct opposition to the way the scientist functions. The only thing that is observable to us is behavior, whether it is verbal or otherwise. From this behavior we infer a process, which we cannot see or measure directly, in order to help us explain the causes of behavior. In other words, although we can see only behavior, we build the linking mechanism which now allows us to explain the entire process. This linking mechanism is known as a construct.

Self-concept, then, is a construct. It has never been seen, nor is it likely that it will ever be seen. As it is used in this book, this term will describe a mechanism which allows us to explain behavior.

Definition

Self-concept, as it is generally used in the professional literature, is a group of feelings and cognitive processes which are inferred from observed or manifest behavior. By way of a formal definition, self-concept is the person's total appraisal of his appearance, background and origins, abilities and resources, attitudes and feelings which culminate as a directing force in behavior. We here hold that a person's conscious awareness, what he thinks and feels, is that which primarily guides, controls, and regulates his performance and action. While it cannot be denied that some people behave without knowing why they behave, this unconscious activity suggests some types of mental illness characteristic of a small percentage of the population. For our purposes, we will be speaking about the person who is aware of his actions and behaviors and knows what he is doing; we will not be referring to those people who are engaged in aimless activity.

How Self-Concept Is Measured

The fact that the self-concept cannot be seen presents severe limitations in determining the state of this factor at any given point in time. If we cannot observe it, how can it possibly be measured? Although it is true that we cannot see the self-concept, we can observe behavior. In this instance, and when dealing with all psychological constructs, one infers the nature of the self-concept from observable behavior over a period of time. The behavior is known to be symptomatic of the problem; therefore, if a person continues to behave in a particular manner, we may infer a linking mechanism from his behavior.

In general, we obtain most of our knowledge about people in this fashion. In order to obtain this information more efficiently, psychometrists have developed a variety of tests to elicit the behavior pattern. Most of these tests require a person to give information about himself, and this may be somewhat limited. However, no one has the continuity of exposure and so continuous an opportunity to observe and evaluate his inner life and thought as the person himself. In order to exploit an individual's likes and dislikes, interests, and attitudes, the obvious approach is to ask him about them. Rogers states: "The best vantage point for understanding behavior is from the internal frame of reference of the individual himself." [1] While the advantage of self-reports is the provision of an "inside view" based on the person's knowledge and experience about himself, there are some definite limitations. This method is weak from the standpoint of possessing external validity. Self-reports can be easily faked unless the goodwill of the subjects is obtained. Some subjects cannot give accurate evaluations of themselves because of emotional blocks or defenses. Also, results may be affected by mood fluctuations or by conditions at the time and place of the testing.

The relative status of a person's self-concept is usually determined through the use of one or more of the following techniques:

1. Introspective self-reflections in personal, family, social, and school or work settings.

[1] C. R. Rogers, *Client-Centered Therapy: Its Current Practice, Implications, and Theory* (Boston: Houghton Mifflin Company, 1951), p. 494.

2. Congruence between descriptions of current self-concept and ideal self-concept.

3. Congruence between subjective self-reports and action and the objective reports of clinically trained observers.

4. Nonintrospective inferences derived from projective techniques and clinical interviews.

On occasions in which a gross incongruity exists between the self-report and the manifest behavior, the veracity of the report is questionable. Benjamins [2] cautions that an individual's statements about himself may not represent how he feels. When the self-report distorts or camouflages the real beliefs and feelings the person holds about himself, we have no accurate measure of the self-concept. It is not merely what a person says about himself, how he describes himself, that can be judged as reliable indicators of expected performance. It is what a person believes he is, what he feels about himself, that directs his behavior. Test instruments can facilitate this kind of investigative study only to the extent that the subject is willing to report his real feelings and beliefs about himself.

Development of Self-Concept

Supporting propositions which respectively explain the development and function of the self-concept are interpersonal and perceptual theories. Although each is presented separately for discussion purposes, they become a unitary theory when applied to practice. That is, interpersonal theory explains the development of self-concept, self-concept selects or limits perception, and behavior and learning are products of perception.

Since the self-concept is inferred from behavior and the behavior is all we ever see, how can we explain why some students attempt a new task with confidence, while others are fearful in attempting it at all? Why is it that some students can accept failure without fear, while others fear to fail? It would be a misconception to view a person with a strong or positive self-concept as one completely without failure or other negative experiences. No one escapes some disappointments and failures. However, the person who is able to deal effectively with these negative onslaughts in life is one whose total

2 J. Benjamins, "Changes in Performance in Relation to Influences Upon Self-Conceptualization," *Journal of Abnormal and Social Psychology,* 45 (1950), 473–80.

economy is essentially positive. When weighed in the balance he feels himself adequate to meet life's challenges because of a sufficient backlog of successful encounters which allows his belief that he is valuable and worthy. One defeat can appropriately be interpreted as "I have failed," not "I am a failure." In observing the behavior of students, one cannot fail to be impressed by the differences of the inner forces which guide behavior, and which we have defined as self-concept. This is not to imply that the process differs for each student; indeed, we do not believe this. Rather, we believe that the process is much the same for all students; it is the *quality* of their experiences which distinguishes those with a good self-concept from those with a poor or weak self-concept.

We believe that the self-concept is built or achieved through accumulated social contacts and experiences with other people. People learn their identity, who and what they are, from the kinds of experiences the growing-up process provides. Sullivan [3] called this development learning about self from the mirror of other people. What a person believes about himself is partly a function of his interpretation of how others see him. Since he really has no way of knowing precisely how other persons see him, he infers this from their behavior toward him. Therefore, his concept of self rests in part on what he thinks others think of him.

The social experiences one has form the basis of one's interaction with others. It is during the formative years that one begins to develop and polish a living style of associating and relating with others. The basic mechanisms of human dynamics are well known and there is no reason to repeat them here. The development of these mechanisms, however, parallels the development of the self-concept. In fact, the mechanisms appear to develop in concert with the self-concept. If a person needs to be on the defensive, for example, he will be very cautious in his relations with others. Kelley states: "The self 'looks out' upon the surrounding scene largely in terms of its own enhancement or defense. It tends to extend in the direction of that which promises to make it better off. It withdraws from that which seems likely to endanger it. This is largely true throughout life and entirely true in the early stages when the self is being established. . . . The more facilitating the environment, the less need for protection. The more endangering the environment, the greater need for protection. . . . Protection (defenses) becomes isolation. The self becomes a prisoner in its own fort. We have all

[3] H. S. Sullivan, *Conceptions of Modern Psychiatry* (Washington, D.C.: William Alanson White Psychiatric Foundation, 1947).

seen persons off whom words or ideas seemed to bounce. They have built their barriers so strongly against other people that they have become inaccessible." [4]

Significant Others

The development of self-concept is particularly affected by the role of "significant others" in the life of a child. At an early age, the most significant others in his life are his parents. How they help him grow and how they react to his exploratory experiences have tremendous influence on him. They are the first people to affect the development of his self-concept, and they continue to be significant others. However, there comes a point in every person's life when he begins to recognize the power and influence of his friends. Although his parents are still important to him, he sometimes feels that they have a legal and moral obligation to love and accept him. His friends, on the other hand, have no such commitment. They will like and accept him for what he is and not out of a sense of duty. When he realizes this, the significant others in his life begin to shift from his parents to his peers. This is not to be construed to mean that his parents cease to be significant others; instead, he increases the number of significant others in his life.

Significant others are the people who most intimately administer the "rewards" and "punishments" in a person's life. Certainly, the classroom teacher should be included in this group. An individual's self-concept is acquired from countless experiences with these significant persons. Also, perceptions of other people are products of learning experiences.

Cultural Influences

In terms of interpersonal theory, the importance of social and cultural influences on self-concept and personality development must not be minimized. Anthropological cross-cultural investigations have clearly demonstrated the impact of socialization practices on personality differences.

Whiting and Child [5] examined the child-rearing practices of some

[4] E. C. Kelley, "The Fully Functioning Self," *Perceiving, Behaving, Becoming,* ed. A. W. Combs (Washington, D.C.: Association for Supervision and Curriculum Development, 1962), pp. 14–15.

[5] J. W. M. Whiting and J. L. Child, *Child Training and Personality: A Cross-Cultural Study* (New Haven, Conn.: Yale University Press, 1953).

seventy-seven cultures. Intensive socialization in all cultures was found to be bound up with the management of aggression, acceptance, independence, sexuality, eating, and toileting. The socialization process was gradual and gentle in some cultures and harsh, punitive, and abrupt in others. They found a reciprocal relationship between the severity of the socialization procedures and the cultural adjustment patterns. Where the socialization was harsh and punitive in childhood, adults were prone to anxiety and guilt, with tendencies to be suspicious of others as potentially hostile. More specifically, abrupt and severe weaning led to an overconcern about food, the suppression of aggression, and guilt about aggressive impulses. An understanding of the dominant cultural patterns of the learning environment gives important clues to the sources of personality formation.

The general patterning of the culture is most profound in terms of resultant influences on personality. Yet, cultural subdivisions such as social-class membership are vitally important in deriving a large part of the child's learning environment. Parental behavior, home factors, the neighborhood and play groups to which one has access are factors of class status.

Havighurst and Taba [6] contrast the formative influences of class membership on values and aspirations. At the risk of some overgeneralizations, the lower-class child puts a premium on immediate gratification in response to his constant uncertainty about such basic matters as food and shelter. In contrast, the middle-class child is enjoined to improve his position by delaying rewards with the prospect of facilitating future achievements. The upper-class child is relieved of the pressures for upward mobility, but has the imposed responsibility of maintaining the reputation of the family and learning proper etiquette, good form, honor, and discretion. In matters of physical aggression, sexual exploration, bodily functions, and habits, there are marked differences among class groups. The restraint criteria of classes have a pervasive influence on the learning environment.

Sociopsychological Theories

In the development of self-concept, heavy emphasis is placed on the theoretical formulations of social psychologists. Adler, Fromm,

[6] R. J. Havighurst and H. Taba, *Adolescent Character and Personality* (New York: John Wiley & Sons, Inc., 1949).

Horney, and Sullivan are eminent proponents of a psychological theory grounded in social processes. A major tenet in Adler's theory is the individual's characteristic response, or "style of life," in relation to his environment. Adler asserts that man constructs his own personality out of the raw material of heredity and experience. "Heredity only endows him with certain abilities. Environment only gives him certain impressions. These abilities and impressions, and the manner in which he experiences them—that is to say, the interpretation he makes of these experiences—are the bricks which he uses in his own creative way in building up his attitude toward life. It is his individual way of using these bricks, or in other words, his attitude toward life, which determines this relationship to the outside world." [7]

The central theme in Fromm's writings is a society which will meet man's basic needs. This society would be one ". . . in which man relates to man lovingly, in which he is rooted in bonds of brotherliness and solidarity. . . ." [8] Fromm states that man realizes his inner potentialities by the social conditions under which he lives. In other words, personality develops in accordance with the opportunities and requirements of the society.

In Horney's theory, the primary concept is that of basic anxiety which disturbs the security of the child in relation to his parents. Horney does not feel that conflict is innate, but rather that it arises out of social situations. "The person who is likely to become neurotic is one who has experienced culturally determined difficulties in an accentuated form, mostly through the medium of childhood experiences." [9] Horney [10] states that people adjust to their anxieties in three main ways: by moving toward people (compliance or love), by moving against people (aggression or power), and by moving away from people (detachment or independence).

Sullivan describes personality development in terms of the individual's interpersonal relationships with his "significant others." Indeed, the individual does not and cannot exist apart from his relations with other people:

[7] A. Adler, "The Fundamental Views of Individual Psychology," *International Journal of Individual Psychology*, 1935, p. 5.

[8] E. Fromm, *The Sane Society* (New York: Holt, Rinehart and Winston, Inc., 1955), p. 362.

[9] K. Horney, *The Neurotic Personality of Our Times* (New York: W. W. Norton & Company, Inc., 1937), p. 290.

[10] K. Horney, *Our Inner Conflicts: A Constructive Theory of Neurosis* (New York: W. W. Norton & Company, Inc., 1945).

The general science of psychiatry seems to me to cover much of the same field as that which is studied by social psychology, because scientific psychiatry has to be defined as the study of interpersonal relations, and this in the end calls for the use of the kind of conceptual framework that we now call field theory. From such a standpoint, personality is taken to the hypothetical. That which can be studied is the pattern of processes which characterize the interaction of personality in particular recurrent situations or fields which include the observer.[11]

Later, Sullivan defines personality as "the relatively enduring pattern of recurrent interpersonal situations which characterize a human life." [12]

Sullivan [13] allows for the fact that one's perceptions may be unrealistic and distorted. After a few months of age, most experiences occur via "parataxic" and "syntaxic" modes. Learning experiences which are unsupported by logic and poorly connected with other perceptions are parataxic experiences. A child whose father is threateningly hostile may generalize this perception to all authority figures. Many of these distortions can be ameliorated by syntaxic experiences which produce logical order. Through "consensual validation" an individual shares the perceptions made by other people as more realistic and standard in meaning.

All these theories emphasize that the person's most important motivations are acquired from his sociocultural situation which is represented by the persons with whom he has significant interpersonal relations. Self-concept is influenced by the relationship a person has at first with his family and peers in unstructured situations and later in more structured situations with teachers and peers. Important for teachers is the fact that self-concepts are not unalterably fixed, but rather are modified by every life experience through at least the maturing years. Inherent in the thought that self-concept is learned as a function of experience is the fact that it can be taught. Interpersonal theory, then, holds that self-concept is built or achieved through accumulated social experiences and contacts.

[11] H. S. Sullivan, "Tensions, Interpersonal and International," *Tensions that Cause War,* ed. H. Cantril (Urbana, Ill.: University of Illinois Press, 1950), p. 92.

[12] H. S. Sullivan, *The Interpersonal Theory of Psychiatry* (New York: W. W. Norton & Company, Inc., 1953), p. 111.

[13] Sullivan, *The Interpersonal Theory,* p. 29.

Perceptual Dynamics of Self-Concept

A necessary interstitial theory for self-concept analysis is perception. Our theoretical persuasion is that a person's self-conception is the principal dynamic in all human behavior. The constituents of self-concept, as noted earlier, are the person's total appraisal of his appearance, background and origin, abilities and resources, attitudes and feelings which culminate as a directing force in behavior. This dynamic causes some students to attempt a task given a minimal chance for success, while others will not attempt a task without a great deal more opportunity for a successful outcome. The self-concept conditions the way students interpret the comments of others toward their behavior and influences also the way they behave in the future in a similar situation. To say that the self-concept is the prime factor controlling all human behavior is not overstating the case. In fact, the self-concept is becoming a more important dimension in the control of human behavior than has been generally realized.

One of the most revealing aspects of perception is that it is a selective process. A person cannot simultaneously register everything in his surroundings. Thus, when a person walks into a room of varying decor, people, and conversations, he is of necessity forced to focus on fewer stimuli than the total number possible. The choices he makes under these circumstances invariably relate to his past experiences as well as to his present needs and current self-conceptions. Perception, then, will be selective in terms of quantity. Furthermore, the individual's self-conception also determines the kind and quality of the experiences he perceives. The concept one has of oneself expands or limits the richness and variety of the perceptions one selects.

We would be naïve to assume that the process of selective perception is a conscious effort. A person does not prepare himself beforehand for what he might select. Instead, as he encounters a situation, certain elements register on him, and he reacts in terms of his past experiences. We are more likely to find evidence of stereotyped thinking in the person who has an extremely limited perceptual field. Preconceived notions of what merely is or ought to be is the root of most prejudicial thought and action. To the person who conceives his civil rights to be in jeopardy, it makes a great deal of difference how he perceives the mystique of "the law." There is little question that people vary in terms of what laws they consider fair and what ones they wish could be ignored. To most participants in a national convention, little thought is given to such matters as enforcement of building and fire laws. To the owners or the managers of such meeting quarters, enforcement may take on a different focus.

Rogers states: "As experiences occur in the life of the individual, they are either symbolized, perceived and organized in some relationship to the self; ignored because there is no perceived relationship to the self structure; denied symbolization or given a distorted symbolization because the experience is inconsistent with the structure of the self." [14] In other terms, it is the individual's self-concept which determines the kind and quality of experience perceived. Perception is selective according to whether the experience is consistent with the current concept of self or not. As a quota system, the self-concept limits openness to experience in only certain consistent and selective ways. Shaffer and Shoben support this proposition: "Because the self-concept shapes new experiences to conform to its already established pattern, much behavior can be understood as a person's attempt to maintain the consistency of his self-concept, a kind of homeostasis at a higher psychological level." [15] Snygg and Combs state that "all behavior is determined by and pertinent to the phenomenal field of the behaving organism." [16] That is, the way a person behaves is the result of how he perceives the situation at the time of his action. It is not the event itself which elicits the specific response, but rather the individual's subjective experience of the event.

As the self-concept develops it brings with it a unique perspective of viewing one's relationship to one's world. What a person perceives and how he interprets what he perceives is conditioned by his concept of self. A person with a weak self-concept and who is unsure of himself is more likely to have a narrowed perceptual field. This shrinking effect limits the data required for intelligent decision and action. The threatened person's perceptions tend to be limited to the objects or events of the threat. This becomes the very antithesis to efficient behavior. Instead of broadening his fund of knowledge and skills, such a person is kept busy defending his already existing perceptual organizations. In contrast, the individual with a positive self-concept is free to devote his energies to the explora-

[14] Rogers, *Client-Centered Therapy*, p. 503.
[15] L. F. Shaffer and E. J. Shoben, Jr., *The Psychology of Adjustment* (Boston: Houghton Mifflin Company, 1956), p. 94.
[16] D. Snygg and A. W. Combs, *Individual Behavior: A New Frame of Reference for Psychology* (New York: Harper & Row, Publishers, 1949), p. 15.

tions and discoveries of the personal meanings of events for him in his world. The positive self has a backlog of actual experiences of acceptance and success. He approaches people expecting to be liked; he engages in activity, expecting to succeed. He feels loved and able as a result of real encounters. Merely being told that one is loved and able is not enough. Strong self-concepts are the result of actual positive experience.

The dynamics of a positive expectation tend to produce the appropriate behavior to bring about the expectation. Whether the person with a weak or strong self-concept is always correct in his expectations is almost irrelevant. As Earl Kelley once observed, "Reality is what one perceives it to be."

Summary

The self-concept is presented as a construct or linking mechanism used by psychologists to infer a process from observable behavior and to help explain the causes of that behavior. We hold that a person's feelings and cognitive processes, of which he has a conscious awareness, are the major components of his self-concept. We further maintain that the individual's self-concept is that which primarily guides, controls, and regulates his performance and action.

Self-reporting is probably the most common means of obtaining a measure of self-concept. Here a subject reports his own inner experiences and feelings. From a pure measurement standpoint, this procedure is somewhat weak in that it does not possess external validity. When the self-report distorts or camouflages the real beliefs and feelings the person holds about himself, there can be no accurate estimate of his self-concept. Despite its subjective nature, the self-report yields evidence that can be obtained in no other way.

The self-concept is built or achieved through accumulated social contacts and experiences with "significant others" during the growing-up process. These "significant others" profoundly affect young people and precondition the development of the self-concept. Significant others are parents, peers, and teachers.

The perceptual selections one makes invariably relate to past experiences as well as to present needs and current self-conception. The concept one has of oneself is also a factor in expanding or limiting the richness and variety of the perceptions one selects. To imply that this process is a conscious effort is to ignore the impact past experiences have on the developing self-concept.

Selected Readings

Anderson, C. M., "The Self-Image: A Theory of the Dynamics of Behavior," *The Self in Growth, Teaching, and Learning,* ed. D. E. Hamachek. Englewood Cliffs, N.J.: Prentice-Hall, Inc., 1956.

Axline, Dibs, *In Search of Self: Personality Development in Play Therapy.* Boston: Houghton Mifflin Company, 1964.

Bills, R., "Believing and Behaving: Perception and Learning," *Learning More About Learning,* Third ASCD Research Institute. Washington, D.C.: Association for Supervision and Curriculum Development, 1959.

Carlson, Rae, "Stability and Change in the Adolescent's Self-Image," *Child Development,* 36 (1965), 659–66.

Costar, J. K., "Some Characteristics of High School Pupils from Three Income Groups," *Journal of Educational Psychology,* 50 (1959), 55–62.

Couch, Carl, and J. Murray, "Significant Others and Evaluation," *Sociometry,* 22 (1964), 502.

Hilgard, E. R., "Human Motives and the Concept of Self," *American Psychologist,* 4 (1949), 374–82.

Jourard, S. M., and R. M. Remy, "Perceived Parental Attitudes, the Self and Security," *Journal of Consulting Psychology,* 19 (1955), 346–66.

Koppitz, E., "Relationship Between Some Background Factors and Children's Interpersonal Attitudes," *Journal of Genetic Psychology,* 91 (1957), 119–29.

Medinnus, G. R., "Adolescents' Self-Acceptance and Perceptions of their Parents," *Journal of Consulting Psychology,* 29 (1965), 150–54.

Rasmussen, G., and A. Zander, "Group Membership and Self-Evaluation," *Human Relations,* 7 (1954), 239–51.

Reissman, L., "Levels of Aspiration and Social Class," *American Sociological Review,* 69 (1953), 233–42.

Rogers, C. R., "Toward Becoming a Fully Functioning Person," *Perceiving, Behaving, Becoming,* ed. A. W. Combs. Washington, D.C.: Association for Supervision and Curriculum Development, 1962.

Chapter 3

OVERVIEW
OF EDUCATIONAL
IMPLICATIONS

What does self-concept theory mean for schools, education, and teaching? What current practices does it question, negate, or support? What new directions does it suggest for curriculum, methodology, and classroom experience?

Self-Concept and the Educative Process

When the child enters kindergarten, he does not arrive as a simplified personality with singular attitudes, ideals, feelings, and traits. Instead, he arrives in a malleable state which is the result of the interaction of many past experiences. It is highly unlikely that these experiences were all similar, that is, that they were all either negative or positive. Rather, it is to be expected that the impact of some of these experiences arose from their competing with some of his other experiences. His present concept of self, and his relationship to the other children and to the teacher, is profoundly affected by such factors as his social-class membership, family structure, parental behaviors, ethnic background, religion, and the language spoken in the home. If his self-concept could be seen at this particular time, it would probably be labeled "developmental" (in-process). Although the child has already developed a concept of himself, he has also experienced the variability of human nature. That is, he knows he may succeed at many of his endeavors, but he should also expect that he might fail to attain some of his goals. At this point, however, his image of himself is not fixed and rigid.

The feelings one develops about oneself are formed quite early in life and are modified by subsequent experiences. The fact that the significant people who come and go in a child's life, leaving an indelible mark on how he views himself, are many and varied leads us to believe that the basic factor in the development of self-image is flexibility. This is perhaps the most important point for the educational practitioner to keep in mind—that the child's self-concept is not unalterably fixed, but is modified by every life experience, both in and out of the classroom, at least through the maturing years. If this were not the case, then we would have to face the alternative of suggesting that there is really little or nothing educators can do to enhance a student's feelings about himself. This premise is self-defeating, because it appears that future success or failure is preordained, that the action one takes will have little impact on what one can become, and that there is a special mysticism surrounding all educational practice. To accept such a premise is to suggest that some people must live with hopelessness and futility, and this denies the basic premises upon which our educational system is built.

On the other hand, the suggestion that teachers are among a number of significant others in a student's life, and that there might be some competition in their influence, is not meant to imply that teachers can take their task too lightly. Exactly how important a teacher can be in the life of any child can be seen in the countless testimonials given each year by people who recall that the most significant person in their lives was their teacher. The opposite is equally true. There are untold thousands who were psychologically maimed by teachers while they were in school. Many of these people have since married and now have children of their own in school. These parents subtly transmit their own fears, anxieties, and hostilities toward school and school personnel to their children. It is little wonder that teachers may have difficulty explaining their function to some parents. A parent who has been hurt by a teacher will jealously guard his child from the onslaught of another teacher.

Evidence of Self-Concept Influences

Empirical and experimental data clearly indicate a direct relationship between the child's self-concept and his manifest behavior, perceptions, and academic performance. Lecky [1] was one of the first investigators to demonstrate that low academic achievement was often due to a child's definition of himself as a nonlearner. Walsh [2] found that "high ability, low achievers" had a negative self-regard when matched with "high ability, high achievers." Benjamins,[3] Reeder,[4] and Buckley and Scanlan [5] presented additional data to demonstrate that a person's self-concept has a direct bearing on his intellectual efficiency.

Brookover, Thomas, and Paterson [6] found a statistically significant positive correlation between self-concept and perceived evaluations of significant others, general performance in academic subjects, and achievement in specific subject-matter fields. Perkins [7] found that teachers who had taken certain courses in mental hygiene and child development were able to promote healthier personality growth in children. Healthy personality growth was defined in terms of the degree of congruence between the real self and the ideal self. Cutler

[1] P. Lecky, *Self-Consistency: A Theory of Personality* (New York: Island Press, 1945).

[2] A. M. Walsh, *Self-Concepts of Bright Boys with Learning Difficulties* (New York: Bureau of Publications, Teachers College, Columbia University, 1956).

[3] J. Benjamins, "Changes in Performance in Relation to Influences Upon Self-Conceptualization," *Journal of Abnormal and Social Psychology*, 45 (1950), 473–80.

[4] T. A. Reeder, "A Study of Some Relationships Between Level of Self-Concept, Academic Achievement, and Classroom Adjustment," *Dissertation Abstracts*, 15 (1955), 2472.

[5] H. Buckley and K. Scanlan, "Faith Enough for Both," *Childhood Education*, 32 (1956), 230–32.

[6] W. B. Brookover, S. Thomas, and A. Paterson, "Self-Concept of Ability and School Achievement," *Sociology of Education*, 37 (1964), 271–78.

[7] H. V. Perkins, "Factors Influencing Change in Children's Self-Concepts," *Child Development*, 29 (1958), 221–30.

and McNeil [8] demonstrated that when mental health consultants worked directly with teachers, the teachers developed greater skill in child management which had beneficial effects for the student indirectly. Davidson and Lang [9] showed that the more positive the children's perception of their teacher's feelings toward them, the better was their achievement and the more desirable was their classroom behavior. In a study of emotionally handicapped children, LaBenne [10] found a highly significant relationship between the teacher's self-concept and the pupil's perception of himself in the classroom.

Self-concept as a factor which influences behavior patterns and adjustment was studied by Martire [11] and Steiner.[12] Both of these investigators found corroborative evidence for a positive relationship between self-concept and social adjustment. Sheerer [13] demonstrated that there was a positive correlation between acceptance of self and acceptance of and respect for others. Stock [14] also found that when a person's feelings about himself changed, his attitude toward others changed in the same direction.

Other researchers have reported finding similar effects of the self-concept on learning and behavior. More important perhaps is the fact that most experienced teachers can recite a great many examples in which a student's conception of his abilities severely restrict his achievement, even though his real abilities may be superior to those which he demonstrates. It is not infrequently that some students will insist they cannot do a task, almost before they have an opportunity to examine the nature of the work. Nor is it unheard of for some students to offer an apology before they answer a question.

8 R. L. Cutler and E. B. McNeil, *Mental Health Consultation in Schools* (Unpublished, Ann Arbor, Michigan, 1963).

9 H. H. Davidson and G. Lang, "Children's Perceptions of Their Teachers' Feelings Toward Them," *Journal of Experimental Education,* 29 (1960), 109–18.

10 W. D. LaBenne, "Pupil-Teacher Interaction in a Senior Ungraded School for Emotionally Handicapped Boys" (Unpublished Ph.D. dissertation, University of Michigan, 1965).

11 J. C. Martire, "Relationship Between the Self-Concept and Differences in the Strength and Generality of Achievement Motivation," *Journal of Personality,* 24 (1956), 364–75.

12 I. D. Steiner, "Self-Perception and Goal-Setting Behavior," *Journal of Personality,* 30 (1957), 344–55.

13 E. J. Sheerer, "An Analysis of the Relationship Between Acceptance of and Respect for Self and Acceptance of and Respect for Others in Ten Counselling Cases," *Journal of Consulting Psychology,* 13 (1949), 169–75.

14 D. Stock, "An Investigation Into the Interrelations Between the Self-Concept and Feelings Directed Toward Other Persons and Groups," *Journal of Consulting Psychology,* 13 (1949), 176–80.

Which teacher has not heard some modification of the comment, "I'm probably wrong . . ." or "This may be a silly question, but . . ."? This type of behavior should be carefully noted, because it might provide, along with additional behavioral evidence, some information about the student's self-concept.

In addition, teachers who gain a measure of intimacy with students can report the many cases in which objectively attractive young people avoid social situations because of subjective feelings of unattractiveness. The point to be made here is that the "facts" as they may seem to an outsider do not necessarily appear to the behaver in the same way. It is not the objective event itself which elicits the specific response, but rather the individual's subjective experience of the event. People react to the same circumstance in different manners, and the way a person behaves is a result of how he perceives the situation at the time of his action. How a person acts and learns is a product of unique and personal meanings, which may, and often does, vary from one person to another.

Educational Influences

In any consideration of the educational implications of self-concept, a relevant aspect is the student's concept of his ability to learn certain types of academic behaviors. Combs points out that the circular effect of a given concept of self is inability to read:

> Such a child is likely to avoid reading, and thus the very experience which might change his concept of self is bypassed. Worse still, the child who believes himself unable to read, confronted with the necessity for reading, is more likely than not to do badly. The external evaluation of his teachers and fellow pupils, as well as his own observations of his performance, all provide proof to the child of how right he was in the first place! The possession of a particular concept of self tends to produce behavior that corroborates the self-concept with which the behavior originated.[15]

Some people have firm images of themselves as people who cannot learn foreign languages, mathematics, statistics, or some other subject. It is an interesting question to ponder whether a person cannot learn mathematics because he does not like it, or whether he does

---

[15] A. W. Combs, "Intelligence from a Perceptual Point of View," *Journal of Abnormal and Social Psychology*, 47 (1952), 669–70.

not like it because he cannot learn it. The answer is academic and not readily apparent, but the two factors appear to vary together; that is, they are correlated. It is probably true that a person's attitude toward a subject is an overriding factor. On the other hand, there is no denying that his attitude is often reinforced by his poor performance. Any attempt to separate these two factors is like arguing over whether length or width contributes more to the area of a rectangle.

These conceptions of an inability to learn appear to be self-fulfilling prophecies. That is, the types of experiences that might alter the notions a student holds about himself are purposely avoided. Instead of obtaining more practice in an area of weakness, the student avoids any further experiences with the subject. The resultant effect is that low-ability level is perpetuated. If, however, for some reason he must take a test or otherwise demonstrate some competency in the area, his attitude will be influenced by his ability, and in this instance both may be rather weak.

Social psychologists clearly state that a person's self-concept is learned through interpersonal encounters with significant others. This becomes a very important dimension of the teaching-learning act, and provides the teacher an opportunity to become a significant other in the life of a student. Any person who is intimately involved in the administration of rewards and punishments is in a position to become a significant other. It is not merely the ability, or responsibility, of administering the system, however, that makes a teacher a significant other. Rather, it is the manner in which he uses his authority that causes him to have a potent impact.

The influence of schooling, in the narrow sense of the term, or education in the broader sense, may have a positive, negative, or neutral effect on a child's concept of self. Whether planned or unplanned, the influence of the school or, more specifically, the teachers, has a great deal to do with the developing self-concept. We should like to examine some teaching activities, therefore, which have specific reference and meaning for the development of the self-image.

Teachers Must Be Honest

We have indicated that people behave in terms of how they see themselves, and this perception in turn influences how things appear to them. The principle implied here is that behavioral change will not occur until the concept of self has been modified. What does this mean for teachers? Some teachers conscientiously avoid making any reference to a student's ability even though they use ability grouping in their classroom. They divide their class into three or four reading groups, call them after a color or species of bird, but never make any reference to the ability level of each of these groups. This game teachers play with themselves amuses the students. Each student is not only aware of which group he is a member, but he is also able to rank-order the groups according to ability. Where ability grouping is used throughout an entire school, the students have little difficulty in distinguishing the various ability levels. A low-ability class once shocked the teacher, because some of the students noted that they were in the "dumb room." This was not said in malice or hurt, but was an honest appraisal. Teachers, however, fear to be as blunt with their students as the students are with the teacher. Instead, they continue to act and treat the class as if each student were identical with the next. They forcefully refrain from making any reference to the varying abilities and other differences among students.

In contrast, another condition which frequently exists in our schools is that teachers take the opportunity to talk with the student about his abilities. During these discussions, it is not unusual for teachers to purposely distort the evidence and go out of their way to provide false praise for poor performance. The student is not fooled by this sham; he knows who he is and what he can do based on actual experience. No passing grade can make him deny his experiences when he must work alongside his classmates each day. This does not mean that the student does not want to get a good grade, or does not want to believe that he is doing his work satisfactorily. Whatever he wants to believe must ultimately be tested against the reality of his experiences. Teachers who behave in this fashion probably do so out of a false notion of kindness. Perhaps they feel that by withholding the truth and providing praise they will not hurt the student's feelings. The kindest approach, however, would be to be completely honest with the students.

When children have the security that the teacher accepts them for what they are as worthy beings, there is no need to give false praise or to disguise the facts with sugarcoating. If children know the teacher is "on their side," they can profit from the truth about their achievements and constructively build upon the knowledge of their needs and current weaknesses. Indeed, there is no other way to assist them in appraising their present progress and establishing next-step plans in terms of what is yet to be accomplished. Confrontation with reality in an atmosphere of warmth and acceptance is imperative for an accurate view of self.

We have in education today something that is known to teachers as "social promotion." It is not our purpose to examine all the pros and cons here, but we would like to examine one instance in which this system might be damaging to children in the developmental stage of self-concept. Many teachers take advantage of this situation to avoid confronting students with their abilities as manifested in their classroom performance. The most they can hope to accomplish by this action is to postpone the reckoning that must come sooner or later. We have seen children in the later elementary grades who have finally had to come to grips with their abilities. Many of these children seemed to believe that they could perform at a level much higher than they actually did. The reason they gave for this belief was that, after all, they had been promoted every year since they entered school. We do not mean to imply here that social promotion is a dangerous process or that it is harmful to students. What we are saying is that it *could* be harmful, and the antidote is for teachers to be honest with students and help them recognize their weaknesses as well as their strengths. Furthermore, teachers must become convinced of the value of rewarding each student for gains that are made in respect to individual desires. There is no reason why students must always be compared to a total class or group. Somewhere in the curriculum and during each day, students must be given opportunities to work to their own expectations, and they should be rewarded when they make significant gains in these endeavors.

It has been said many times before that "Nothing succeeds like success." This, however, does not mean that we can tell a student he is doing well when he is not. This axiom can be made operational only when teachers provide meaningful activities in which students can explore and discover the personal meaning of events for themselves. To do this demands that teachers know the students and select for them experiences that provide, at a minimum, the opportunity for success. Studies in achievement motivation have documented that when the task is seen as being virtually impossible of attainment, there is no shame in failure. Where the task is viewed as being ridiculously easy, there is no desire to perform. The most adequate tasks, in terms of incentive and satisfaction, are those which contain a probable chance of success. The mandate is clear: To help a child develop a positive self-concept, one must help him select experiences which provide a challenge, and at the same time help him maximize his opportunities for success.

This mandate is more easily said than done, because it demands a clear recognition that there can be no predetermined standards for an entire class. Each student must be viewed as a separate entity and learning tasks must be tailored, insofar as possible, for each student even though the entire class is being taught at the same time. To insist that class standards exist is not only to ignore the fundamental principles of child growth and development which state that each child grows, develops, and learns at differing rates, but is also a clear distortion of the concept of a class average. A class average is obtained by a statistical consideration of the performance of all the students. This means that some students are above average and some are below. If all students were performing at a high level, then the class average would be higher, but there would still be some students above and below the average.

Predetermined Decisions

One of the most damaging and vicious practices in our public schools today is the tendency on the part of some teachers to make judgments about a student on the basis of his cumulative record, without ever having seen the student. This practice denies the student any credit for growth that might have been made during the summer months. Furthermore, it often reinforces the bias of the preceding teacher without an opportunity to collect the evidence firsthand. Teachers might be further ahead if they did not avail of the opportunity to view the cumulative record until after the first marking period. This approach would force them to base their evaluations on behavioral evidence rather than hearsay. Perhaps this procedure would be unnecessary if all teachers really believed that it was their function "to take the child where he is," but unfortunately this is not the case. The many years that this slogan has been preached by professors of education has had relatively little impact on teachers. For some strange and undefined reason, there is a great deal of security in following a lock-step curriculum.

Many teachers cry out to be creative and innovative, but surprisingly few are willing to provide similar opportunities for their students. What teachers fail to recognize is that quite often students know more about the teacher than he knows about the students. The well-developed grapevine works most effectively among students. We recall quite vividly a second-grade teacher who conducted a unit on chickens each year. It was amazing to observe the responses of children upon learning that they would be in her room for the following year. Although they knew almost exactly what she would do, they all wanted to go through the experience themselves. There are two points to be made here: (1) the students enjoyed the security of knowing what would be forthcoming, and (2) although they knew in advance what the teacher would do, they never behaved in a manner to force her to modify her teaching.

Students certainly deserve every bit as much consideration as teachers themselves. Even if a teacher knows firsthand about a student, he has an obligation to give the student a fair trial when he arrives in the new class. To classify him on the basis of another teacher's experience with him is to do a grave injustice to the student and to make a mockery of the word "education."

Students Become What They Are Thought to Be

The teacher who believes in the fixed or static character of pupil abilities, interests, traits, and values is quite likely to convey this attitude and provide experiences that maintain and perpetuate these same self-concepts. If a teacher believes that a student is a failure, he may provide him with experiences so shallow that he could not possibly fail. The challenge will not be there, and the student will view it as "mickey mouse." Or, the teacher may not adjust the program to the pupil's abilities so that he will consistently do less well than other students. In either case, the student will soon learn that he does not belong. If he is provided with failure after failure, we can expect that sooner or later he will come to believe he is a failure and will act like one.

None of us would long continue to drive a car if each time we got into a car we also got into an accident. Sooner or later we would run out of excuses and begin to believe that we are "accidents about to happen." The same is true of children: they cannot long tolerate consistent failure without having something happen to them. Indeed, what happens is that they begin to see themselves as being persistent failures in school and are just waiting for the time they can leave school. These students are psychological dropouts long before they become physical dropouts. The evidence is mounting to support the theory that dropouts are made in the elementary school, not in the secondary school. When they do finally leave school (which, because of compulsory attendance, is quite likely to be the high school), their departure will be based on a decision that was a long time aborning; it will not be a hastily made decision.

As we said earlier in this chapter, the student entering school is malleable; his self-concept is in the process of developing. How teachers treat him and react toward him becomes a factor in how he views himself. Experiences may cause him to become locked in a certain stage of developmental progression. The consequence is tragic for the child who happens to be slower at the onset of his academic career. The student who is seen by his teachers to be handsome but slow, brilliant but careless, average but mischievous, talented but lazy will behave accordingly. Until a student is presented with other evidence and experiences, he will remain incarcerated in these pockets of self-concept.

Summary

In this chapter the central place of the teacher as an agent influencing the developing self-concept of the student is emphasized. Numerous studies indicate a direct relationship between the child's self-concept and his manifest behavior, perceptions, and academic performance. The manner of the teacher in presenting the subject matter is of critical importance, because teaching activities have specific reference and meaning for the development of the student's self-concept. Some of these activities are internalized by the student as being self-defeating, and the circular effects of these conceptions reinforce an inability to learn certain kinds of academic material.

The need for honest student appraisal and evaluation, while at the same time avoiding comparisons with other students, is a necessity. Confrontation with reality in an atmosphere of warmth and acceptance is imperative if one is to get an accurate view of self. False praise for poor performance is seen by the students as a sham. Here it is emphasized that students must be provided real experiences in which they can have success and from which they can draw the inference that they are successful.

The common practice of establishing pre-set standards for groups of children is viewed as frankly damaging to the self-concepts of many individual children within the group. Teacher expectancies and goals for the student must be set individually; each student must be provided experiences that are in concert with his own particular inventory of abilities, needs, and interests. That these traits are transient should have meaning for the teacher in terms of his classroom techniques. The teacher who believes in the fixed or static character of pupil abilities, interests, traits, and values is likely to convey this attitude to the students and provide experiences that maintain and perpetuate these same self-concepts.

Although the practice of using cumulative records and hearsay as a basis for student evaluations is not unusual, one would hope that current behavioral evidence would be more influential in determining the evaluation. It is difficult to argue with the idea of using all available evidence, but the teacher cannot overlook the fact that last year's information may be out of date. Nor can the teacher forget that this information may be biased. Students have a right to expect that they will be judged on their current performance, not on what other teachers think of them.

Selected Readings

Andrews, R. J., "The Self-Concept and Pupils with Learning Difficulties," *Slow Learning Child,* 13 (1966), 47–54.

Bruck, M., and R. F. Bodwin, "The Relationship Between Self-Concept and the Presence and Absence of Scholastic Underachievement," *Journal of Clinical Psychology,* 18 (1962), 181–82.

Combs, A. W., *The Professional Education of Teachers.* Boston: Allyn and Bacon, Inc., 1965.

————, "Intelligence from a Perceptual Point of View," *Journal of Abnormal and Social Psychology,* 47 (1952), 662–73.

Fink, M. B., "Self-Concept as it Relates to Academic Under-Achievement," *California Journal of Educational Research,* 13 (1962), 57–62.

Hamachek, D. E., *The Self in Growth, Teaching, and Learning.* Englewood Cliffs, N.J.: Prentice-Hall, Inc., 1965.

Holt, John, *How Children Fail.* New York: Pitman Publishing Corporation, 1964.

Hott, L., and M. Sonstegard, "Relating Self-Conception to Curriculum Development," *Journal of Educational Research,* 58 (1965), 348–51.

Morse, W. C., "Self Concept in the School Setting," *Childhood Education,* 35 (1964), 195–201.

Roth, R. M., "Role of Self-Concept in Achievement," *Journal of Experimental Education,* 27 (1959), 265–81.

Samler, J., "The School and Self-Understanding," *Harvard Educational Review,* 35 (1965), 55–70.

Sears, P., and V. S. Sherman, *In Pursuit of Self-Esteem.* Belmont, California: Wadsworth Publishing Company, Inc., 1964.

Shaw, M. C., and G. J. Alves, "The Self-Concept of Bright Academic Underachievers: II," *Personnel and Guidance Journal,* 42 (1963), 401–3.

Shaw, M. C., K. Edison, and N. R. Bell, "The Self-Concept of Bright Underachieving High School Students as Revealed by an Objective Check List," *Personnel and Guidance Journal,* 39 (1960), 193–96.

Stevens, P. H., "An Investigation of the Relationship Between Certain Aspects of Self-Concept, Behavior, and Students' Academic Achievement," *Dissertation Abstracts,* 16 (1956), 2531–32.

Wattenberg, W. W., and C. Clifford, "Relation of Self-Concept to Beginning Achievement in Reading," *Child Development,* 41 (1964), 461–67.

Chapter 4

THE MEANING
OF INTELLECTUAL
FUNCTIONING

One of the major contributions to education in the twentieth century has been the advent and progress of psychological testing. This is not to imply that differences among students were not recognized before the appearance of psychological testing; it does mean that the beginnings of accurate and scientific measurement were not undertaken before the turn of the century. Prior to the development of psychological testing, students were sorted by other means. Plato, in his *Republic,* provided for a sorting and sifting process whereby children would be prepared to become warriors or philosophers or artisans. Throughout the history of education, people concerned with the educational process have sought means of sorting students which would not be so subjective.

The major breakthrough came in 1905 when Alfred Binet was requested by the Minister of Public Instruction in Paris to develop a means of identifying children who were mentally unfit for school. Binet collaborated with Simon, and together they sought to find empirical evidence about children's behavior which might be called intelligence. They began with questions and relatively simple tasks that tested common sense and judgment within the experiences common to all children of a given age and culture, and found that they could differentiate between children based on their ability to perform these tasks. For example, they found that certain tasks that could be performed by eight-year-old children could not be done by seven-year-olds. In this manner, they devised a test for the various age levels. If a ten-year-old student could not perform the tasks usually mastered by eight-year-olds then he was obviously below average. Conversely, if an eight-year-old performed the tasks required of ten-year-olds, he was above average.

A revision, in 1908, contained the concept of mental age, and thus the I.Q. was born. This test was imported by Henry Goddard, given an English translation, and standardized for use with American children. Revised by Terman in 1916, it became known as the Stanford revision (Stanford-Binet). This basic test, which was last revised in 1960, is perhaps the most widely used individual intelligence test in the country today.

Intermittently, since the introduction of intelligence testing, these tests have been under fire. Much of the confusion, debate, and outrage has centered on whether the tests measure innate or inborn intellectual capacity and potential. Many thought the data were too inaccessible and varied to be measured precisely. Others felt that education must be concerned, not so much with what existed, but with what was yet to come. That is, education must be concerned with emergent learnings and not with the child as he is now.

Neither Binet, nor the psychologists who revised his tests, Cattell, Goddard, and Terman, believed or claimed to measure a fixed, unchanging intellectual ability. There appears to be an implicit assumption, however, in Binet's work; namely, that children who have been slow or fast in developing will probably continue to develop at a similar pace. Thorndike, furthermore, put forth the argument that what could not be measured could not be known, and that what exists, regardless of amount, could be measured. Thus it was that these early efforts came to mean that we could test constancy of endowment. Unfortunately, many teachers and parents got the notion that intelligence could be directly measured by instruments capable of testing results adequately, and that the native potential of the individual could be accurately predicted. Evidence of this misunderstanding of the ratio between mental age and chronological age is seen in the common interchangeable use of "I.Q. test" and "intelligence test." These terms are not synonymous; they never have been and never will be.

Individual and Group Testing

Until now we have been talking about the Binet test, which we have noted is an individually administered test. The chief advantage of such a test is that it is given to one student at a time by a professionally trained psychologist or psychometrician. This person is sensitive to a student's lack of motivation to complete the test, his language handicap, or some emotional disturbance which can render the results invalid. In an individual-testing situation, too, a trained person can observe functioning intelligence, which is almost impossible to measure and which is imperceptible under group-testing conditions. For these reasons, individual tests are said to be more valid than group-administered tests.

For practical and economic reasons (the individual-testing situation is too time-consuming and too expensive), however, group tests that seek to provide the same kind of information have been constructed. Much of the data found in school records today comes from these standardized tests which can be administered to large groups of people and which require a less highly trained specialist. Unlike the individual tests, group tests are essentially paper-and-pencil instruments in which students respond to written instructions. Thus, the majority of these tests depend heavily on language ability.

Unquestionably, the greatest misuse of the concept of intelligence came with the paper-and-pencil tests introduced in the 1920's. While they have the expedient quality of mass administration to large groups of students, they have none of the advantages of the professionally administered individual tests. In fact, the recent decision of the New York City schools to discontinue the use of group-intelligence tests was based largely on charges that these tests were unfair to "disadvantaged" children. Loretan, in discussing the reasons for the discontinuance of such tests, quotes Clark as saying that I.Q. scores based on the usual group-administered tests "are worse than meaningless; they are misleading." [1]

Intelligence—a Hypothetical Construct

The meaning of the term "intelligence" has never been made very clear. Most modern psychologists concur that intelligence is a hypothetical construct inferred from observable behaviors. That is, intelligence is not capable of being measured directly, but is judged from samples of a person's ability to perform. Performance implies that intelligence is more a process than a product, more of what one does than what one has, more an idea of "I will" than "I.Q." Generally, the performance areas examined by intelligence tests are perceptual acuity, discriminatory activity, and use of symbols in problem solving. More specifically, some forty kinds or types of mental abilities have been identified by Guilford and his students. No doubt, many more types are yet to be properly identified. One of the major dangers in the use of intelligence tests is the tendency for teachers to look at the summation score, or I.Q., as an appropriate indication of all-around performance. Of much more value are the subtest scores which point to strengths or weaknesses in specified areas: relative ability to deal with concepts, principles, symbols, social situations, manipulative aspects of things, and so forth.

In discussing the definition of intelligence, Horrocks and Schoonover say:

> It is difficult to define intelligence. Attempts to define it encounter the real danger of giving intelligence, in the thinking of the definer, a kind of corporal existence that places it in the category of a real entity that can be isolated and examined. A definition of intelligence makes it easy to forget that "intelligence" is merely a word to indicate those behaviors, significant in human existence, which psychologists and others have come to call intelligence.[2]

Therefore, rather than hang a quantitative label on an individual's intelligence, a look at the kind and quality of intelligence is de-

[1] J. O. Loretan, "The Decline and Fall of Group Intelligence Testing," *Teachers College Record*, 67 (1965), 10–17.

[2] J. E. Horrocks and T. I. Schoonover, *Measurement for Teachers* (Columbus, Ohio: Charles E. Merrill Books, Inc., 1968), p. 282.

sirable. Since intelligence is an activity, not an entity, it behooves us to examine the person's ability to perform certain kinds of activities. It takes a certain kind of intelligent behavior to be a mechanic, a secretary, a teacher, or a medical doctor, and few people are intelligent in their performance of all these behaviors.

Hereditary Influences

Interminable debate on the extent to which intelligence is restricted or expanded by inheritance and environment persists. That nature and nurture are inextricable components of intelligence seems axiomatic. Certainly, intact cerebral hemispheres are a requisite for intelligent behavior, but exactly how knowledges, skills, and experiences are mediated in the brain is still an academic question. On the other hand, the fact that bread turns into blood is also particularly vague. No matter how operationally perfect the digestive system may be, it is useless without nutrients. No matter how gifted, superior, or talented the mental inheritance, it is wasted without learning opportunities and experiences. The extent to which intellectual endowment is inherited is not the vital consideration for educators, because whatever the native inheritance, educational provisions can enhance it. Except in the cases of gross organic pathology, the capacity to learn and profit from experience is not concentrated in any one type or level of intelligence. All people can learn.

The idea that the I.Q. is a satisfactory measure of a person's intrinsic intellectual prowess is nothing short of the naïve. This naïveté leads to unwarranted boasting of mental superiority and ultimate achievement in later life when high scores are produced, to lack of personal worth and assumptions of unteachability when low scores are produced. That intelligence tests are fairly reliable instruments in the prediction of present capacity to succeed in learning the kinds of things required in school in no way justifies the notion that innate ability or potential is measured. Perhaps what we should learn from the correlations of I.Q. scores and school performance is that the traditional experiences provided in school are unsuitable for the child measuring low in such tests. What the tests really measure is essentially scholastic aptitude. Although definitions of intelligence have been numerous, none has proved satisfactory. No doubt, this is why some have disdainfully concluded that "intelligence is what intelligence tests measure."

Environmental Influences

If a Wechsler-Bellevue, Stanford-Binet, or one of the many group-intelligence tests was administered to an Australian aborigine, the likelihood is that he would have an "idiot" I.Q. On the other hand, it is quite conceivable that the aborigine could devise an instrument to measure practices and customs of his native culture which would give the average American a similar "idiot"-level intelligence. The African Bushman's conception of snow or the Eskimo's conception of walls and certain degrees of angularity might be deficient, because the individual's previous opportunities for learning and actual exposure to environmental events profoundly affect his capacity for effective behavior.

Apart from the comparatively few cases of physical limitations in intellectual development (mongoloids, cretins, organic impairments), what environmental deprivations or stimulations affect intellectual abilities? Snygg and Combs [3] define the phenomenal field as the universe of experience open to the individual at the moment of his behavior. It is reasonable to assume that the extent to which one's opportunities and experiences are limited or expansive, the extent to which one's perceptual field is distorted or clear, to the same extent will one's manifest intelligent behavior be efficient or inefficient. The individual's intelligence then is dependent upon the quality of the perceptions available to him.

Numerous studies over the last fifty years show a general trend of positive correlations between intelligence-test results and opportunities provided by the environment. Inferior-tested ability is found in rural rather than urban children, in orphanages rather than homes, in low socioeconomic status rather than high, in Southern rather than Northern states, in ghettos, mountains, and everywhere children live in isolation from educational opportunity, richness, and variety. The relative deprivation or stimulation in terms of creative playthings, travel, books, parental aspirations, goals, values, and interests influences the breadth and quality of the child's perceptual field.

At this time a principle can be stated which generalizes the environmental influences on intellectual performance: The greater the length of time a child lives in a given environment, the greater

3 D. Snygg and A. W. Combs, *Individual Behavior* (New York: Harper & Row, Publishers, 1949).

the likelihood that his I.Q. will approximate the characteristic level of that environment. This is no longer a postulation, but an empirically tested hypothesis. A number of experimental investigations which support this principle are cited in the references at the end of this chapter. Almost miraculous rises in I.Q. scores have been reported in cases where withdrawn children were placed in environments of affection and understanding. Marked improvements in children with "low I.Q.'s" have occurred when they were put into a warm, loving relationship, especially when mothers and fathers were also involved.

Other Important Factors

One cannot overlook the importance of many factors other than the I.Q. in relation to education today. It is only recently that creativity has received some attention as an important dimension of the educational process. The dependence of the I.Q. as the sole measure of giftedness has shocked many educators doing research in this area. Now we are beginning to recognize that there may be many kinds of giftedness other than that measured by the I.Q. There have been several research efforts in support of the work of Getzels and Jackson [4] to document that the I.Q. and creativity scores are not related or are related only to a low degree. Thus, the use of only an I.Q. score may distort the information sought about students.

The major contribution from research on creativity is a recognition that the I.Q. may be a good measure of academic potential, but is of little use in predicting job success. Taylor and Barron [5] found that college grade-point average did not distinguish among the ratings employees received. One thesis is that our educational system today teaches people to memorize and recite the past, but does not prepare them to develop new things for themselves. This means that they are far better able to perpetuate the past than to improve upon it.

It is almost impossible to discuss the issue of intelligence at the present without recognizing the impact of the works of Torrance

[4] J. W. Getzels and P. W. Jackson, *Creativity and Intelligence* (New York: John Wiley & Sons, Inc., 1962).
[5] C. W. Taylor and F. Barron, *Scientific Creativity: Its Recognition and Development* (New York: John Wiley & Sons, Inc., 1963).

and Guilford. Torrance [6] has developed tests for the assessment of creativity, and his research has often been cited for the use of creativity as well as achievement and I.Q. to determine school programs. Guilford's structure of intellect construes the intellect along three dimensions which include four kinds of contents, five kinds of operations, and six kinds of products, or a total of one hundred and twenty combinations of abilities. This means that although several students may have the same or similar I.Q. scores, they each may have arrived at this point along different roads. Guilford also reminds us that "those who search for simple answers and for a single key to unlock the door to the understanding of the intellect will be disappointed." [7]

We do not wish to belabor the issue or to elaborate on the important works cited above, because these efforts require far more attention than we can give here. Our reason for introducing them is to illustrate some of the changes currently being considered when discussions of "intelligence" or "gifted" students are undertaken. Certainly, these efforts are forcing educators to modify the singularity of their approach toward working with students. It is in this regard that we find relevance in the research cited.

In addition to some of the factors mentioned above, there are some correctable physical defects that affect mental performance. On the surface, it seems that the energy available to utilize intelligence is related to a nutritious diet. Harrell [8] noted marked improvement in mental alertness of children with thiamine deficiencies when additional amounts of thiamine were given to them. Kubala and Katz [9] found a significant gain in low I.Q. children when they were given increased ascorbic-acid concentrations. Apparently, both physical and intellectual ability are closely related to diet—at least where specific deficiencies are found.

Opportunities to experience events are usually severely limited by sensory deficits. Impaired hearing creates difficulty in the association of sounds with written words. Competency in judging spatial relationships is reduced by visual defects. The inability to experience tactile stimulation, to distinguish colors, or to taste and smell will

[6] E. P. Torrance, *Guiding Creative Talent* (Englewood Cliffs, N.J.: Prentice-Hall, Inc., 1962).

[7] J. P. Guilford, *Personality* (New York: McGraw-Hill Book Company, 1959), p. 395.

[8] R. F. Harrell, "Mental Response to Added Thiamine," *Journal of Nutrition*, 31 (1946), 283–98.

[9] A. L. Kubala and M. M. Katz, "Nutritional Factors in Psychological Test Behavior," *Journal of Genetic Psychology*, 96 (1960), 343–52.

isolate the victim from many learning opportunities. When these limitations are not corrected, or the school experiences modified to meet the uncorrectable defect, the intellectual development and realized ability of these children are greatly reduced.

Relationship to Self-Concept

Perceptual psychologists have developed the plausible theory that people more often than not do what is expected of them, and they become what they are thought to be. This is so because the reflected image a person sees of himself in social contacts and experiences with significant others, as well as with their expectations of his performance, help establish the self-concept. As we have indicated earlier, the formation of the self-concept depends upon two factors: (1) how a person perceives he is judged by significant others, and (2) a comparison of these judgments against a standard that he holds on how he should behave. Thus, his own judgment is constantly modified by his perception of the judgment of others. In other words, he is testing his perception against the reality of an external criterion.

What is a difficult, and perhaps dangerous, activity is that a teacher should view the I.Q. as a static quality of ability and adjust his teaching to that level. It is then that the I.Q. becomes a self-fulfilling prophecy. This posture of maintaining and perpetuating a given level affects not only the teacher but also the student. Thus, the judgment of the student about his abilities is modified by his perception of his teacher's judgment of his abilities. In a real sense, the student is testing a hypothesis about his ability with an external criterion. The possibility that the teacher may be wrong does not enter the scene even remotely. This, indeed, is one of the dangers of which teachers must be aware, because it can become manifest in the development of a negative self-concept.

Loretan maintains that "good teaching and increased student motivation" can elevate the I.Q. He reports that children in the New York Demonstration Guidance Project gained an average of 15 points in I.Q. tests, with the range being a gain of 5 to 40 points. Thus, with proper help, I.Q. and achievement tests reveal a noticeable increase. Loretan says: ". . . there is the sense that the new programs may counteract the fatalism fed by beliefs of inherent inferiority, based on misinterpretations of the meaning of the I.Q." [10]

[10] Loretan, *Teachers College Record*, p. 14.

Another interesting report by Rosenthal and Jacobson [11] describes the testing of the hypothesis that teachers tend to see the child through his I.Q. and adjust academic expectations accordingly. In this study, the researcher chose the names of pupils at random and told their teachers that the pupils' academic performance would dramatically improve during the school year. The only difference between the randomly selected group and the other students was the suggested improvement for the former and the resultant more favorable teacher expectations for that group. The results indicated that the experimental group improved an average of 27 I.Q. points compared to 12 for the other students in the first grade, and across-grades improvement favored the experimental group 12 points to 8.

If we as teachers consider intelligence as a fixed individual capacity, we will teach, grade, and evaluate in such a manner as to corroborate the student's conception of his level of ability as measured by tests. Our behavior will then maintain the student's present concept of his ability and reduce the chance of change in his concept of self. Combs states: "If, in our schools, we teach a child that he is unable and if he believes us and behaves in these terms, we need not be surprised when we test his intelligence to discover that he produces at the level at which we taught him." [12]

Summary

There are no test instruments yet devised which can accurately measure the native intellectual potential of the individual. Although these instruments can provide gross estimates, they do not measure drive, diligence, and desire. Unless this is understood, there is a calculable danger in the misconceived notion that a fixed, unchanging intellectual endowment can be presently measured. The best of these instruments are those which are administered individually. Because the mass-administered paper-and-pencil tests are dependent on reading skills and individual motivation, they are the least valid.

Intelligence, like so many other psychological terms, is a construct. As such, it is not possible to measure it directly, but rather it is judged from samples of a person's ability to perform. Per-

11 R. Rosenthal and L. Jacobson, *Pygmalion in the Classroom* (New York: Holt, Rinehart and Winston, Inc., 1968).
12 A. W. Combs, "Intelligence from a Perceptual Point of View," *Journal of Abnormal and Social Psychology*, 47 (1952), 670.

formance implies that intelligence is a process, not a product; an activity, not an entity; what one does, not what one has. The kind and quality of intellectual behavior (functioning intelligence) is more useful to the teacher than the quantitative label expressed in a summation I.Q. score. The capacity to learn and profit from experience is not concentrated in any one type or level of intelligence.

That intelligence tests are fairly reliable instruments in the prediction of present capacity to succeed in learning the kinds of subject matter required in school in no way justifies the notion that innate ability is measured. That some students score low on these tests may simply be an indication that the traditional experiences provided in the schools are unsuitable for these students.

It is reasonable to assume that the extent to which one's opportunities and experiences are limited or expansive, the extent to which one's perceptual field is distorted or clear, to the same extent will one's manifest intelligent behavior be efficient or inefficient. In addition to the deprivations of a restricted emotional and intellectual environment, there may be some connectable physical defects which affect mental ability.

If we, as teachers, consider intelligence as a fixed individual capacity, our behavior will likely help produce and maintain the student's conception of his abilities as measured. If this were to happen, we would have reduced the chance for the student to change his self-concept of his abilities. The burden of this responsibility on the teacher is awesome and cannot be taken lightly.

Selected Readings

Asher, E. J., "The Inadequacy of Current Intelligence Tests for Testing Kentucky Mountain Children," *Journal of Genetic Psychology*, 46 (1935), 480–86.

Bledsoe, J. C., "Self-Concepts of Children and their Intelligence, Achievement, Interests, and Anxiety," *Journal of Individual Psychology*, Vol. 20 (1964).

Bowman, D. O., "A Longitudinal Study of Selected Facets of Children's Self-Concepts as Related to Achievement, Intelligence, and Interest," *Dissertation Abstracts*, 24 (1964), 4536–37.

Burks, B. S., "The Relative Influence of Nature and Nurture Upon Mental Development: A Comparative Study of Foster-Parent Foster-Child Resemblance and True Parent-Child Resemblance," 27th Yearbook, *National Society for the Study of Education*, Part I (1928), pp. 219–316.

Combs, A. W., "Intelligence from a Perceptual Point of View," *Journal of Abnormal and Social Psychology*, 47 (1952), 662–73.

Crissey, O. L., "Mental Development as Related to Institutional Residence and Educational Achievement," *University of Iowa Studies in Child Welfare*, Vol. 13 (1937).

Gordon, H., "Mental and Scholastic Tests Among Retarded Children," *Educational Pamphlet #44*. London: Board of Education, 1923.

Haggerty, M., and H. B. Nash, "Mental Capacity of Children and Paternal Occupation," *Journal of Educational Psychology*, 15 (1924), 559–72.

Hilgard, E. R., "Creativity and Problem Solving," *Creativity and Its Cultivation*, ed. H. Anderson. New York: Harper & Row, Publishers, 1959, pp. 162–80.

Honsik, M. P., J. W. McFarlane, and L. Allen, "The Stability of Mental Test Performance Between Two and Eighteen," *Readings in Child Behavior and Development*, ed. C. Stendler, 2nd ed. New York: Harcourt, Brace & World, Inc., 1964, pp. 467–69.

Hunt, J. McV., *Intelligence and Experience*. New York: Harcourt, Brace & World, Inc., 1962.

Husen, Torsten, "The Influence of Schooling Upon I. Q.," *Theoria*, 17 (1951), 61–88.

Jones, H. E., "The Environment and Mental Development," *Manual of Child Psychology*, ed. L. Carmichael. New York: John Wiley & Sons, Inc., 1954.

Kagen, J., et al., "Personality and I. Q. Change," *The Causes of Behavior*, eds. J. Rosenblith and W. Allinsmith. Boston: Allyn and Bacon, Inc., 1962, pp. 297–302.

Skodak, M., and H. M. Skeels, "A Follow-up Study of One Hundred Adopted Children," *Journal of Genetic Psychology*, 66 (1945), 21–58.

Torrance, E. P., *Guiding Creative Talent*. Englewood Cliffs, N.J.: Prentice-Hall, Inc., 1962.

Wiesen, H. H., "An Investigation of Relationships Among Intelligence, Organizational Climate in the Classroom, and Self-Concept as a Learner Among Ten and Eleven Year Olds," *Dissertation Abstracts,* 26 (1966), 6520–21.

Yarrow, L. J., "Separation from Parents During Early Childhood," *Review of Child Development Research,* Hoffman and Hoffman, eds. New York: Russell Sage Foundation, 1964, pp. 89–136.

Chapter 5

THE ISSUE
OF ABILITY
GROUPING

Educational administrators, theoreticians, and teachers have been "groping for grouping" for at least four decades in the concern to improve the educational provisions for all students. There are myriad articles, surveys, and sentiments recorded in the professional literature, together with descriptive accounts of various practices and programs relating to ability grouping. An examination of much of this literature reveals it to be of irregular quality, and the results inconclusive and somewhat confusing.

What Research Says About Grouping

The practice of grouping students, already widespread by the 1920s and 1930s, traces its origins back to the previous century. W. T. Harris' plan, initiated in St. Louis in 1867, is often cited as the first attempt at homogeneous grouping. Under this plan, groups of bright students were chosen by their teachers on the basis of achievement and promoted rapidly through the elementary grades. A few years later, Elizabeth, New Jersey, inaugurated a somewhat similar plan, with classes of bright pupils formed from each of the elementary grades and moved through the program as rapidly as possible. The Cambridge, Massachusetts, plan came into operation in 1891, with the pupils so grouped that the brightest might complete grades four through nine in four years, while the slowest took seven or eight years. The Santa Barbara Concentric Plan was adopted at the turn of the century, with each grade being divided into A, B, and C sections, and each section mastering the same fundamentals for each subject, but the A's doing more extensive work than the B's and the B's more than the C's. These and other plans—the Newton Plan, the "Double Tillage Plan" of Woburn, Massachusetts, the New Richmond (Wisconsin) Plan—are just a few of the dozens of schemes for flexible progress and promotion which were in operation sufficiently long to merit attention in the professional literature.

It was not until 1916 that any serious attempt was made to study homogeneous grouping with something resembling controlled experimentation. Guy M. Whipple studied a gifted class consisting of thirteeen boys and seventeen girls chosen on teacher recommendation from fifth and sixth grades of an Urbana, Illinois, school. Whipple's can be regarded the first scientific study of ability grouping. Numerous other studies followed soon after, with the greatest number occurring in the late 1920s. By the early 1930s, several good summaries and critical reviews of the research appeared.

Billett reviewed one hundred forty articles, including one hundred eight experimental or practical studies that appeared in the literature between 1917 and 1928. Of these one hundred eight studies, Billett listed one hundred two as uncontrolled, two as partly controlled, and four as thoroughly controlled. Of the one hundred two uncontrolled studies, eighty-three were favorable to grouping, ten were doubtful, and four were unfavorable. One of the partly controlled studies was favorable to grouping, the other was doubtful. Two of the four thoroughly controlled studies were favorable to grouping, one doubtful, and one unfavorable. Among the trends in the study of homogeneous grouping, Billett found the general recognition that "so-called homogeneous grouping in practice produces not homogeneity, but reduced heterogeneity." [1]

Turney in his analysis of the research on grouping concluded that ". . . most of the studies purporting to evaluate ability grouping have proved nothing regarding ability grouping, but have only added evidence bearing upon the nature and extent of individual differences." [2]

Twenty studies were summarized by Miller and Otto in 1930. Their conclusions were that while the evidence was contradictory, at least two of the studies suggested that ability grouping was quite ineffective unless accompanied by proper changes in methods. As for achievement, furthermore, there was no clear-cut evidence that homogeneous grouping was either advantageous or disadvantageous.

The National Society for the Study of Education, in its 35th Yearbook (1936), presented a comprehensive discussion of the practical, theoretical, and experimental considerations in grouping pupils as of that time. Cornell's chapter on the "Effects of Ability Grouping Determinable from Published Studies" included an examination of findings related to (a) academic achievement and speed of learning; (b) quality of learning; (c) intellectual traits and habits of work; (d) social, emotional, and personal adjustment; and (e) health and creative interests. Cornell concluded:

> The results of ability grouping seem to depend less upon the fact of grouping itself than upon the philosophy behind the grouping, the accuracy with which the grouping is made for the purposes intended, the differentiation in content, method, and speed, and the techniques of the teachers, as well as upon more general environmental influences. Experimental studies have in general been too piecemeal to afford a true evaluation of the results, but when attitudes, methods, and curricula are well adapted to further adjustment of the school to the child, results, both objective and subjective, seem favorable to grouping. [3]

[1] R. D. Billett, *Provisions for Individual Differences, Marking and Promotion,* Bulletin 1932, No. 17 (Washington, D.C.: U. S. Government Printing Office, 1933), p. 6.

[2] A. H. Turney, "The Status of Ability Grouping," *Educational Administration and Supervision,* 17 (1931), 122.

[3] E. L. Cornell, "Effects of Ability Grouping Determinable from Published Studies," *National Society for the Study of Education,* 35th Yearbook, Part I (Bloomington, Ill.: Public School Publishing Co., 1936), p. 304.

A review of the literature on experimental studies of homogeneous grouping by Ekstrom in 1959 resulted in finding thirteen studies that showed differences favoring homogeneous grouping, fifteen that found no differences or found grouping detrimental, and five that gave mixed results. Additional conclusions were: no consistent pattern for the effectiveness of homogeneous grouping was found to be related to age, ability level, course contents, or method of instruction; experiments that specifically provided for differentiation of teaching methods and materials for homogeneous groups, and that made an effort to "push" bright students, indicated that homogeneous classes tended to favor the homogeneous groups.

Even as the number of grouping studies has accumulated over the past three decades, the inconclusiveness of research findings becomes more apparent as each reviewer couches his summary in tentative or equivocal terms. While it is true, as Ekstrom observed, that the studies differ widely in quality, purpose, and significance, there are also many other differences that make synthesis of research in this area difficult. The conflicting findings of Cornell led her to observe that ". . . a review of the objective results of ability grouping leaves one convinced that we have not yet attained any unequivocal experimental results that are capable of wide generalization." [4]

Thus it is that the research evidence does not provide a clear answer on the effects of ability grouping, but does allow one to draw one's own conclusions. Those who argue in favor of ability grouping cite one set of statistics, while those who argue the opposite point of view quote from entirely different sources. We are no different ourselves; we hold that ability grouping and the methods it employs are detrimental to the development of a positive self-concept. We should like to explain why we believe this.

Our Point of View

The longitudinal method of obtaining perspective on child development is enlightening. While we can speak with certainty about an orderly sequence of developmental tasks (sitting before standing), the rate and pattern of growth spurts and plateaus emphasizes the need to use the individual child as his own standard. All efforts to reduce the range of differences in children over a sustained period of time are failure-oriented. Whether we group children on the basis

4 Cornell, *National Society,* p. 290.

of age, achievement, or mental tests, wide differences still persist. Olson's [5] survey of grouping practices indicates that children learn in accordance with their unique and personal abilities and the experiences provided for them, irrespective of how they are grouped. If we could actually standardize a group of children at the beginning of a semester, we would soon find a wide variation as the semester progressed. There is no real escape from a classroom or group of variable students. Nor should there be! Many lay people fail to recognize that the purpose of education is not to serve as the "great leveler" of individual differences, but to increase the differences among students. Those who see education as a leveling agent are disregarding the richness of diversity and ignoring the essence of growth. We not only should recognize differences, but we should work toward increasing these differences among students. A quality education that is to provide for the unique growth of each student will increase rather than decrease the differences among students.

The task of the teacher, then, must be to meet individual differences rather than attempt to eliminate them. Failure to understand and accept these fundamental principles of development frequently leads to unwarranted rewards for the rapidly growing child and unfair punishment for the slowly growing child. These are the actions on the teacher's part which hinder the normal development of self-concept. It is also unfortunate to observe that many problems for children are school-produced by maintaining standards at a time that the child is still unable to meet them. Inflexible standards will leave the capabilities of the fast child unchallenged and lead him into false feelings of satisfaction and superiority. The slow child, on the other hand, unable to digest the same diet, meets with frustration and failure. An extensive survey of ability-grouping practices by Cook [6] demonstrates that growth is not stimulated by ability grouping at all. Indeed, school achievement is simply learning at a specified time of child readiness, rather than learning on a predetermined schedule. This should not be construed to mean that teachers must merely wait until a student is ready to learn. What it does mean is that teachers must be able to recognize when the child is ready, and provide appropriate activities for him at that time. In the case of the student who is not yet ready, teachers have been taught a variety of activities designed to stimulate dormant

[5] W. C. Olson, *Child Development* (Boston, Mass.: D. C. Heath and Company, 1959).

[6] W. W. Cook, *Grouping and Promotion in the Elementary School* (Minneapolis, Minn.: University of Minnesota Press, 1941).

readiness. Some of these activities can be observed in any nursery, kindergarten, or preschool.

One of the most frequently expressed concerns of teachers is how to motivate the child. Inherent in this concern is the idea that motivation is to be externally manipulated, that the child is inert and directionless, or worse still, that the child will seek wrong or damaging experiences. A view of human motivation more in keeping with present knowledge is that man has a built-in need and will for self-fulfillment and adequacy. Furthermore, he will naturally seek from his environment those experiences consistent with this motivation. Experiments enumerated by Jersild [7] demonstrate that when offered a choice of good foods infants will choose those that make a balanced nutrition. Ault,[8] Jenkins,[9] and Lazar [10] present studies in the self-selection of reading and arithmetic materials which also indicate the natural desire for growth appropriate to the child's ability and interests, and his needs.

All children are always motivated, but not necessarily to do what the teacher has established arbitrarily as their need. The concept of motivation is useful to the teacher when he views it as the child's *seeking behavior*. Thus aware, the teacher will not try to control or coerce, but rather see the seeking behavior as a signal of the child's readiness for an experience. Here the teacher's task is to provide a wide perceptual field from which the child can draw, and to pace the child's readiness with appropriate stimulation for learning. Each grade can have materials of varying difficulty in order to provide every child successful experiences at his level of development. As a child proves he has attained facility at a given level and is ready for the next level, he will then move. This can be done at any time it is deemed necessary, not at a specified time in January or June. Individual levels must be compatible with present achievement regardless of age, and curriculum revision should occur according to sequential growth to accommodate changing student needs. The indirect advantage of child movement from level to level as he is ready is that it requires teachers to analyze and evaluate constantly, not merely at report-card marking or end-of-year promotion

[7] A. T. Jersild, *Child Psychology* (Englewood Cliffs, N.J.: Prentice-Hall, Inc., 1960).

[8] B. C. Ault, "The Use of the Self-Selection Principle in the Teaching of Arithmetic" (Unpublished Master's thesis, University of Michigan, 1945).

[9] M. Jenkins, "Here's to Success in Reading: Self-Selection Helps," *Childhood Education*, 32 (1955), 124–31.

[10] M. Lazar, "Individualized Reading: A Program of Seeking, Self-Selection, and Pacing," *Reading in Action*, 2 (1957), 141–44.

time. Learning theory clearly indicates that people continue to strive when success is within their grasp. The child wants for himself the adequacy the teacher wants for the child—something not often appreciated.

Some mention should be made here of the ungraded or nongraded school, because it appears that this is what we have been talking about. The concept of the nongraded school is exhilarating, but when viewed in actual practice it is discouraging. In most schools where ungrading takes place, students are literally grouped according to reading or some other ability, and movement from one level to another is at a minimum. The evidence to date suggests that students achieve more, read more widely, and are better adjusted in the graded classroom than in the ungraded.[11] Ungraded classes would surely provide opportunity for our suggestions.

Effects of Grouping on Self-Concept

The basic principles of perceptual psychology present themselves as plausible explanations of the learning process and preferred styles of learning. The essential tenets are that a person learns as a result of personal exploration and discovery of the meaning of events for him; that learning modifies behavior; that one must perceive differently before one can behave differently; and that the feelings and beliefs one holds about self, induces selectivity or restriction in what is perceived and how it is interpreted. This view suggests that the learning process is highly individual and unique for each student. No two people can perceive or feel in exactly the same way. The traditional method of "tell 'em and test 'em" ignores the very personal nature of what is meaningful to individuals. To say "I'll learn them" is not only grammatically incorrect, but is a psychological impossibility. Information and knowledge will not modify behavior unless they are perceived as meaningful to the learner. Therefore, the only "real" teacher lies within the learner—learning is self-appropriated. Educators, at best, can be leaders in learning by stimulating current needs and facilitating the pupil's quest for personal discovery about self and how he relates to the world of events.

On the basis of the foregoing considerations, we might formulate

[11] D. Moore, "Pupil Achievement and Ability Grouping in Graded and Ungraded Primary Schools" (Unpublished Ph.D. dissertation, University of Michigan, 1963).

a guiding principle: Children must be provided with continuous educational experiences adjusted to individual rates of development, needs, interests, and personal meanings. In our opinion, ability grouping appears to be alien to this principle. What are some of the effects of ability grouping on children?

When children are grouped according to ability, there is a tendency to establish and reinforce the individual's concept of his ability in the particular area, and to perpetuate it from that time. After the third year of this differential placement, the child seldom breaks from this rank.[12] The child incorporates the teacher's judgment of his current status and begins to behave as expected. In other words, the child is brainwashed; he is taught a lie about himself which fixes his potentialities, and is locked in a compartment of ability. Teachers who recognize the negative effects of grouping on some children have sometimes attempted to camouflage the ability aspects of groups. But children and parents inevitably identify the group and the status, or loss of status, associated with grouping. One second-grade teacher who used euphemistic disguises for reading groups was disconcerted to have a parent report that her son had announced, "I'm in the 'Space-Bound' group for dumb readers."

Luchins and Luchins [13] examined children's attitudes toward grouping. They found that children are not only aware of the differences when several ability groups are created within a grade, but strongly desire to be in the highest group. In addition, children feel that their parents expect them to achieve higher-group status, and that ability grouping prevents them from making free choices of friends. For many parents, the child's success becomes the parent's reward. Parents often express to teachers their dissatisfaction with their child and sometimes with the school if the child is not in the top-ability group or placed in programs for the gifted. These desires and anxieties of parents are passed on to their children, sometimes in not too subtle a manner. Their concerns are expressed in the form of demands that the child be more diligent and serious and achieve a higher level. Siblings are pressured to work harder to maintain the prestige achieved by others. Perceptual psychologists conclude from these observations and theoretical considerations that ability group-

[12] A. W. Combs, "Intelligence from a Perceptual Point of View," *Journal of Abnormal and Social Psychology*, 49 (1952), 562–73.

[13] H. I. Luchins and E. H. Luchins, "Children's Attitudes Toward Homogeneous Groupings," *Journal of Genetic Psychology*, 72 (1948), 3–9.

ing leads to stereotyped and stratified school roles and parental pressures which prevent the child from developing healthy social relationships and positive self-concepts.

A large-scale study by Borg [14] investigated a number of academic and personality variables as they relate to ability and random grouping for children ranked as superior, average, and slow. He found that random grouping favored concepts of self, acceptance of self, feelings of belonging, and reduction in antisocial tendencies for all ranks. While ability grouping slightly favored achievement scores for the students ranked as superior in elementary school and those ranked as superior and average in the junior high school, there was a negative relationship for all the students ranked as slow. Borg remarks that the achievement differences over the four years were small. This study points up a most important issue. It is far easier to measure academic achievement than self-concept (see Chapter 9). That is why most studies relating to ability grouping use gains in academic performance as the major criterion. It is entirely possible, however, that while a student is gaining in academic performance he is losing something in his development of self. In the light of the Borg study, then, ability grouping is a questionable practice for academic concerns, and appears to be frankly unfavorable for the child's developing personality.

Grouping and the Exceptional Student

There is little question that some gross and severe cases of physical, social, or mental deficiencies require segregation or isolation from regular classes. Some exceptional children need teachers with special skills and training, and special facilities. But a close, hard look at policies of special placement for many exceptional children is needed. Let us now consider the effects of regular-class placement for some types of exceptionality. The effects of segregated and partially integrated school programs on the educable retarded child's self-concept and achievement were studied by Carroll.[15] After eight months of half-day regular-class placement, the retardates in this setting had a significant decrease in self-derogations. The retardates

14 W. R. Borg, *Ability Grouping in the Public Schools* (Madison, Wisc.: Dembar Educational Research Services, 1966).
15 A. W. Carroll, "The Effects of Segregated and Partially Integrated School Programs on Self-Concept and Academic Achievement of Educable Mental Retardates," *Exceptional Children*, 34 (1967), 92–99.

who were segregated and had no school contact with normal children were significantly more derogatory of themselves. In the area of reading, the retardates attending half-day regular classrooms made significant improvement over those in the segregated setting. Studies by Elenbogen [16] and Thurstone [17] also support the hypothesis that educable retarded children make more academic growth in a regular classroom than do those in a segregated classroom. Even in the absence of these investigations, the rationale might still be for regular-class placement with programs adjusted for individual differences so that the child can become accustomed to living with the total environment. After all, the educable retardate does live in a heterogeneous world and will eventually work there. For many of these children, the only time they will be labeled "retardate" and be forced to live apart is during the school years. This labeling and segregating has a negative effect on the developing self-concept as indicated in the study by Carroll cited above.

Many teachers want emotionally disturbed children segregated from the regular classroom, because they believe that the disturbed child contaminates the ongoing process of learning. They fear his misbehavior demands too much of the teacher's time, and that his conduct has a contagious effect on the behavior of others. Kounin, Friesen, and Norton [18] studied teaching styles that affect the behavior of emotionally disturbed children in the regular classroom. They found that teachers who were successful in managing normal behaviors were also successful with the disturbed child, and that these successful teachers not only contained the misbehavior of the disturbed child, but prevented it from disrupting the other children's behavior. While there is little doubt that some teachers would like these children placed in another room, the fact is there are other teachers who must endure the exceedingly difficult task of facing an entire classroom of such children. It would be far easier to have one or two disturbed students scattered in each class than to have all of them in any one class. In this manner, the teacher will be in a better position to work effectively with such

[16] M. Elenbogen, "A Comparative Study of Some Aspects of Academic and Social Adjustment of Two Groups of Mentally Retarded Children in Special Classes and Regular Classes," *Dissertation Abstracts*, 17 (1957), 7496.

[17] T. G. Thurstone, "An Evaluation of Educating Mentally Handicapped Children," Special Research Project, Report No. OE-SAE-6452 (Washington, D.C.: U. S. Government Printing Office, 1959).

[18] J. S. Kounin, W. V. Friesen, and A. E. Norton, "Managing Emotionally Disturbed Children in Regular Classrooms," *Journal of Educational Psychology*, 57 (1966), 1–13.

students. Placing them all in one class almost precludes the possibility of any one teacher being able to devote individual attention to these students.

Ability Grouping and the Gifted

Traditionally, gifted children have been ignored and bored, accelerated or double-promoted, or given enriched programs within the regular classroom or specially grouped with others of like ability. The grouping of gifted children appears to be based on a false premise: they are alike. Gifted children are not a homogeneous group: there are great differences in home and family backgrounds, temperaments, past experiences, interests, and creative abilities. Some educators contend that segregation of the gifted is unnatural and undemocratic because not only are gifted students when grouped deprived of certain opportunities such as leadership (they are more often than not the value setters, value models, and value enforcers in an integrated setting), but "other-ability" students also are denied this positive influence. Segregation, they argue, does not give the gifted sufficient opportunities to associate with other children where mutual respect and understanding for the contributions of varying abilities can develop. Thus, the segregated gifted child sometimes loses perspective of what his competencies really are, because he associates only with his intellectual equals. In this setting, he is likely to develop a distorted sense of "averageness," and in many cases the gifted one simply has to work harder to get average marks in a competitive situation. This point is illustrated in the case of high schools that have honors classes. In many instances, the student in an honors class is in a more competitive position than the student in a regular class. Even a student at the top in a regular class may be only "average" in an honors class.

In discussing the development of the concept of self, we are not considering any particular group of students; we are discussing students in general. The talented student who finds himself in an honors class and who is not doing as well as he might in a regular class suffers in his development of self-concept to the same extent as do his friends who are not as talented. If such a student is forced to compete with the "best" students, in all probability he will not be the top student. In this situation, he is forced to question his self-image with reference to his classmates. Nowhere is he helped to understand that if he does not do as well in an honors class as he did in a regular class, it is not because he is stupid, but rather because of the difference in competition. Some experience with this condition leads us to believe that a student would prefer to have a good grade outright than know he got a "C" in an honors class.

Acceleration

Acceleration refers to the process of moving the child through school at an earlier age than is normal—that is, telescoping or skipping grades. Apart from the possible "halo effect" of such adjustment, it would seem probable that skipping any grade leaves definite learning gaps. Learning cannot be narrowed to the limits of academics only, but must include social and emotional development as well. An inherent flaw of acceleration is that instead of covering a continuous sequential program of studies in a shorter period of time, the gifted child simply works at tasks established for "average" children who are older than he. By acceleration, in effect, we merely adjust the child to the school, whereas our purpose should be to adjust the school to the needs of the child.

Another form of acceleration is early admission to kindergarten or first grade. Still another kind is to provide opportunities, at the high-school level, for students to enter college with advance credit. This is generally accomplished by providing college-level instruction while the student is still in high school. Following the course of instruction, the student may elect to take an examination in the material. Many colleges generally accept these scores in lieu of one or more semesters of college work. Thus, the student will have stayed with his own age group while pursuing studies that are in concert with his academic ability.

Enrichment

Enrichment is based on the belief that educational experiences should be paced according to the child's ability. In terms of the gifted student, provisions for depth penetration of given assignments may be satisfactory as enrichment. Here, students may be given the opportunity for independent research, leadership responsibilities, or creative pursuits. Busy work, however, is not enriching, and activities that enhance further learnings must be carefully selected. Again, in all types and at all levels of ability, a wide selection of books, materials, and equipment is essential. In addition to depth learning, opportunities should be provided for personal discovery and interest projects.

At this point, it may occur to the reader that enrichment has universal applicability, irrespective of the child's mentality. This is true. If we have as our basic commitment the provision of appropriate educational experiences for each child according to his unique abilities and interests and needs, then the grouping of children is no longer defensible. We all learn from one another by exploring and discovering differences, and by sharing them. For example, in a comprehensive study of forty-five New York City elementary schools, Goldberg, Passow, and Justman [19] examined the effects of ability grouping. They found that classes that included all ability levels generally had superior attainment to that of other specified grouping patterns. They concluded that the presence of gifted students, regardless of the ability range of the class, had a positive effect on the nongifted students in both achievement and personality factors such as self-attitude, interests, and school attitude.

Our Position on Ability Grouping

Since children learn the experiences they live, the natural, heterogeneous world seems the most appropriate place for them to gain the experiences needed for future life. In the real world, natural grouping is based on interests more than any other factor. When teachers form groups, their abilities are likely to be varied, but their interests unify them. So, too, there are times when children may unite over a common-interest project or experiment or report, where each can contribute and receive according to his individual ability. Indeed, one might reasonably expect that children will also learn to appreciate the limitations and capabilities of others unlike themselves.

It is difficult for many teachers to conceive of dealing with the variety of ability levels generally found in the classroom. These teachers fear that they will not be able to present their material in such a manner as to reach all the students. They naïvely believe that it is possible to group students and therefore have a class of students with similar abilities. In the first instance, this kind of grouping is not possible. Students grouped for one subject will likely be un-

19 M. Goldberg, A. W. Passow, and J. Justman, *The Effects of Ability Grouping* (New York: Teachers College, Columbia University, 1966).

grouped for any other subject. Second, we feel that since the evidence is not in favor of ability grouping, it is educationally questionable. We cannot, however, overlook the fact that many teachers want ability groups. This means that teachers, too, want to be accommodated; and they have a good point here. If it were not for the probability of unfavorable consequences for the students, we should have no objection. Under the present circumstances, however, ability grouping may be a most dangerous practice.

The insistence on instructional arrangements, such as grouping, is based on conditions that existed in a pretechnological society where the major purpose of the teacher was to transmit information. If the teacher now conducts the learning experience by talking or otherwise performing in front of his class, heterogeneous grouping is unsatisfactory—no matter how beneficial it may be to students in areas other than the academics. The plain fact is that we are now entering the age in which technological innovation can make individualized instruction a reality, in which teachers are not the only vehicle for the delivery of information, and in which machines can offer relief from many burdensome and unimportant tasks. In the future, the role of the teacher will be dramatically changed from an agent of transmission to a director of learning activities. The transmission of information can be done by other media, and teachers will be freed to focus their attention and skill on helping students use the information they are learning.

Teachers may, understandably, be reluctant to forego ability grouping. If, however, we consider some of the dangers and damages that seem to be inherent in intellectual segregation, we cannot condone this practice. When we look at the difficulty of one teacher attempting to meet the individual needs of variable students, we realize the need to organize more effectively for instruction. Have we perhaps set an unrealistic goal for teachers when we subscribe to the concept of individualized instruction? All the evidence in the psychology of development and learning emphasizes the need to educate children according to their own readiness and needs. And yet, we have not found a way to accomplish this, so that lip service is about as far as we have gone in this area. Today we may be on the threshold of developing the procedure for accommodating the individual differences we have talked about so long.

In addition to the accommodation of differences in the classroom through use of the new technology, existent differences may be advantageously exploited to the benefit of the entire class. Sometimes the most effective teachers of children are children. Children have been teaching their peers songs and games for centuries. Perhaps we could guide this natural teaching into more specific areas. It may be possible for the teacher to tutor a "slow" child in a new lesson and then send him into a larger sector for child-to-child tutoring. In this setting one might occasionally find the slow child explaining something new to the gifted child. Not only would this occurrence reinforce the learned material for the slow child, but it would also enhance his feelings of personal worth, at the same time allowing him to provide a worthwhile service. Meanwhile, the slow child might be motivated to try harder simply by observing the brighter child perform a more sophisticated task.

The evidence is far from conclusive, and the research done in this area allows each person to draw his own conclusions. Our position, based on the evidence of research, our knowledge of human development, and our philosophical persuasion, is that ability grouping can and does cause damage to the developing self-concept. We believe that if we educate every student according to his own inventory of abilities, interests, and needs via individualized instruction, we will have obviated the need for ability grouping and the attendant dangers therein.

Summary

In this chapter it is argued that the need for ability grouping is obviated when teachers adjust tasks and expectancies to individual students. There are a number of research studies that indicate that children learn in accordance with their unique and personal abilities and the experiences provided for them, irrespective of how they are grouped. Since wide differences persist regardless of whether or not students are grouped, or the basis on which they are grouped, the task of the teacher is to meet individual differences rather than attempt to eliminate them.

On the premise that human motivation gives man a built-in need and will for self-fulfillment and adequacy, curriculum revision is urged to accommodate the "seeking behavior" of the students. The teacher's role is to provide a wide perceptual field from which the student can select. More important perhaps is the need to pace the student's readiness to move from any given level of attained facility by offering sequential educational experiences. Furthermore, it is maintained that the only "real" teacher lies within the learner, and the feelings and beliefs he holds about himself induce selectivity in what is perceived and how it is interpreted.

Based on the foregoing considerations, ability grouping appears to be alien to the principle that students must be provided with continuous educational experiences adjusted to individual rates of development, needs, interests, and personal meanings. An inherent danger of ability grouping is that the student might well incorporate his current status as fixed potential, and therefore be locked in a compartment of ability. Ability grouping also appears to lead to stereotyped and stratified school roles and parental pressures which prevent the student from developing healthy social relationships and a positive self-concept.

A number of studies indicate that the regular class (random grouping) favors concepts of self, acceptance of self, feelings of belonging, and reduction of antisocial tendencies for all students—exceptional and "normal." Since students learn what they live, the natural world of heterogeneity seems to be the most appropriate educational experience for them.

Selected Readings

Association for Supervision and Curriculum Development, *Learning More About Learning,* Third ASCD Research Institute. Washington, D.C.: The Association, 1959.

Association for Supervision and Curriculum Development, *Freeing Capacity to Learn,* Fourth ASCD Research Institute. Washington, D.C.: The Association, 1960.

Clark, D. H., and G. S. Lesser, *Emotional Disturbance and School Learning.* Chicago: Science Research Associates, 1965.

Della-Dora, D., *One Hundred Years of Grouping Practices.* Detroit, Mich.: Wayne County Board of Education, 1960.

Dyson, E., "A Study of the Relationship Between Acceptance of Self, Academic Self-Concept, and Two Types of Grouping Procedures Used with Seventh Grade Pupils," *Dissertation Abstracts,* 36 (1965), 1475–76.

Ekstrom, R. B., *Experimental Studies of Homogeneous Grouping.* Princeton, N.J.: Educational Testing Service, 1959, p. 19.

Goslin, D. A., "Accuracy of Self-Perception and Social Acceptance," *Sociometry,* 25 (1962), 283–96.

Gowan, J. C., "Changing Self-Concepts in Exceptional Children," *Education*, 85 (1965), 374–75.

Mayer, C. L., "The Relationship of Early Special Class Placement and the Self-Concepts of Mentally Handicapped Children," *Exceptional Children*, 33 (1966), 77–81.

Michigan Association for Supervision and Curriculum Development, "How Grouping Practices Affect Learning," MASCD Series, IMPACT EDUCATION, #1.

Sears, P. S., "Levels of Aspiration in Academically Successful and Unsuccessful Children," *Journal of Abnormal and Social Psychology*, 35 (1940), 498–536.

Turney, A. H., "The Status of Ability Grouping," *Educational Administration and Supervision*, 17 (1931), 21–42, 110–27.

Chapter **6**

PROMOTION
PRACTICES

The American teacher today faces an almost insoluble dilemma when the time comes to decide whether or not a student should be retained in grade. This is not a very palatable situation for any teacher to face, and the decision, whatever it is, is never made lightly. Still, the situation has to be faced; and the problem has to be solved somehow. The decision, however, does not come forth easily, because it is bound up with a much deeper issue that has found no resolve.

Past Promotion Practices

American education today is based on values that are competing and opposite. The two basic values to which we refer are excellence and equality. These two values are difficult of resolution, because they are not really compatible in our schools. Basic values were not an issue when our educational system started. There was little reason to query the purposes of education. It was a system geared to the needs and desires of an elite class, and it was not necessary to be concerned about those who could not make it. In other words, everyone knew the objectives of the system, and those who entered it implied that they would follow the rules that had been established. Under this type of system, it was believed there was a stated amount of "knowledge" to be gained at each grade level. Therefore, a student who could not pass the subject matter in one grade could not expect to progress to the next grade. The utilization of such a system, of course, implied that the instructional program was logically and sequentially planned; and that any year's subject matter was to be based on what was covered the preceding year. Without these assumptions, the logic of the system is faulty.

Of course, one had to be prepared to make many sacrifices under such a system. There could be no exceptions; students who could not perform at an acceptable level were not to be promoted. That this approach might cause some difficulties was not to be an overriding factor. That many students might not be able to perform at the desired level meant that something was wrong with the student and perhaps he really did not belong in school. That students grew older and were forced to work with younger children was of little concern to school personnel. The upshot was that there were many students who were three and four years behind grade level. This was viewed as the fault of the student; he was the one who was failing and he knew what was necessary to make appropriate gains. If he was not capable of this, then he really had no business in school.

It was common to fail a student in the belief that a repetition of work would lead to subject-matter mastery. Threat of failure was used with the expectation that the pupil would work harder. However, according to research findings, neither failure nor threat of failure produced the desired results. Failing and retaining a student in the same grade was fruitless if not damaging. Indeed, there was a greater tendency for the retained pupil to do less well during the year after retention than he had done on comparable tests the year previously.[1]

Retention Not Conducive to Pupil Welfare

As researchers began to focus on the question of whether or not to promote, some issues became obvious. The students who had been retained in grade did not appear to perform any better than they did the first time around. Goodlad [2] reports a study conducted over a two-year period by Arthur in which students who were retained in grade were matched by mental age with those who were promoted. The results showed that there were no differences between the groups in terms of how much they learned. In the same article, Goodlad discusses a study by Kleve and Branson in which all the students who would usually have been retained were matched according to sex, mental age, and chronological age and were then divided into two groups. One group was promoted while the other was retained. The conclusion was that, in terms of achievement, the students who were promoted profited more than those who were retained.

The evidence began to mount in support of the belief that non-promotion did not contribute to excellence. Not only was it demonstrated that students did not profit academically from this policy, but the side effects were even more negative. Retained students did not appear to put forth their best effort. Rather, they seemed to assume a negative attitude toward school. Repeaters tended to select their friends from their own age groups, and these students were often in higher grades. Furthermore, the personal and social adjustments of the nonpromoted students were lower than those of the promoted.

Perhaps the most profound aspect of failure was its detrimental effect on the emotional welfare and social adjustment of pupils. The retained students were much more likely to quit school than those regularly promoted. Other findings demonstrated that the nonpromoted children were less acceptable to their peers and had

---

1 See Selected Readings: Coffield and Blommers, Hall and Demarest, Otto and Melby.

2 J. I. Goodlad, "Some Effects of Promotion and Nonpromotion Upon the Social and Emotional Adjustment of Children," *Journal of Experimental Education*, 22 (1954), 301–28.

greater difficulty in making satisfactory social adjustments than their classmates of the same ability. Finally, the retained children became increasingly antagonistic, with concomitant difficulty in peer-pupil and teacher-pupil relationships.

Providing Equality

Another serious issue that cannot be avoided in any discussion of promotional policy is the question of educational equality. We have indicated earlier that excellence and equality are competing values and are not compatible in our schools. When the commitment for all children to have a secondary education was made, it became necessary to forsake the rigors of an absolute standard of performance because educators acknowledged the obligation to serve all youth. If an absolute standard were to be maintained, this would mean that many students would fail and not be eligible for promotion. On the other hand, if our schools were to provide educational experiences for all youth, it would be necessary to modify the curriculum. In order to provide for the diversity of abilities, the schools added courses such as shop, home-making, dramatics, vocal music, art, typing and shorthand, and other business subjects. Thus it was possible for students to elect a vocational or a business curriculum in addition to the college preparatory curriculum.

The commitment to provide every American child with an education through the high school introduced many problems. Teachers were no longer secure in being under the impression that every pupil was there to learn. Many pupils were in school because the law said they had to be there; they were not there by choice. Furthermore, teachers were faced with the unusual task of having to work with pupils of wide-ranging abilities. It was incumbent on the teacher to find methods and materials to accommodate all the pupils. This was not an easy task, and even to this day, we have not adequately resolved the issue. One need only look at the literature relating to the disadvantaged child to realize that the profession has not been sufficiently responsive to the challenge. Many changes have been made, texts and other materials have been revised, and some teachers have employed creative techniques of teaching these pupils. But by and large, the demand for more suitable materials and teaching methods is still with us. We can never forget, nor should we, the commitment we accepted when we joined the profession.

Now, if we recognize differing ability levels, and if the evidence regarding nonpromotion is valid, do we have no choice then but to promote? In the past, it was common to resort to a simple scheme of "social promotion." After many years of following this procedure, however, it must be concluded that it has not proved a good solution. Perhaps the reason for this is that many teachers viewed retention as a form of curriculum adjustment. That is, the student demonstrated that he could not perform satisfactorily at one level and that, therefore, he obviously would not be able to perform at a higher level. This argument makes sense, of course, only when the curriculum is constructed in such a fashion that each course is built on the preceding course. This is not the case. However, the real dilemma is that we have rejected nonpromotion as a form of curriculum adjustment, but we have not found a workable substitute. In the secondary schools, we provide a choice of curricula. This is one form of adjustment. But no matter what the curriculum, no matter what the standards of performance, there will always be some pupils who cannot make it. What of them? Can we fulfill our noble obligation to provide equally for all if we neglect these pupils? And if we do not neglect them, how shall we provide for their unique abilities? The answer is not simple and is as yet unknown. Certainly, retention is not the answer, but does social promotion resolve the issue? The choices open to teachers today are too limiting; they are either self-defeating or passing the buck. In any case, it would seem that, with regard to the problem of promotion, the alternatives have not been clearly delineated.

Promotion and Self-Concept

What is of interest to us mainly is, how does all this relate to self-concept? If our basic premise is accepted, namely, that self-concept is the key to human behavior, then promotion or nonpromotion must be viewed in terms of the impact it has on the developing concept of self. When students view nonpromotion as a degradation and impugning of their abilities, it is not too difficult to see how they are affected and made to feel. To what avail, then, is it to retain a student in the hope that he will do better, if the result is that he begins to see himself as one who "can't" perform? The reinforcement of this self-concept does not promise improvement; rather, it can be expected that new problems will be created. One need only look at the statistics for those who drop out of school to learn that most of the dropouts had been retained at least once in their school careers.

This is not to say that if a student is retained he will be a dropout; other factors are also important. At the same time, however, we cannot deny the evidence that many students who do leave school before completion were retained at some point in their educational careers.

An analysis of experimental data from a variety of sources allows us to suggest that there is a causal relationship between nonpromotion, on the one hand, and achievement, personal and social adjustment, and dropping out of school, on the other. Placing the self-concept in the chain of causative factors leads us to suggest that nonpromotion is a step in the development of a poor self-concept; and a poor self-concept may lead to withdrawal from school. No matter how valuable and beneficial an educational experience might be, those who cannot find success and security in this endeavor must find a way out. It is not too difficult to appreciate this position. If one cannot succeed in school, there is no reason to accept the continual ego bombardment that takes place. One would be much better off to get out of that situation and into one in which one can compete more favorably. Jersild [3] suggests that each of us must protect the self-concept we develop no matter how illusory it may be. Therefore, one seeks to find an environment that is compatible with one's beliefs.

Competing Systems

There is yet another important factor in this chain, one that deals with the social legitimacy of youth. Our nation has no really useful purpose for our young people. They cannot gain employment until they reach a certain age; therefore, school is the only socially (and legally) legitimate occupation for them. Those of us engaged in education, though, generally live in two worlds—the real world and that which exists within the four walls of the classroom. The latter world is usually no less unreal for the student either; we make it real for him only to the extent that we give it meaning. For the most part, then, students are obliged to work out their educational "occupation" caught between two worlds. The difficulty they are faced with stems from the fact that the models, expectancies, rewards, and punishments of the school world differ greatly from those of the real

[3] A. T. Jersild, *In Search of Self: An exploration of the role of the schools in promoting self-understanding* (New York: Bureau of Publications, Teachers College, Columbia University, 1952).

world, and students are hard put to reconcile these differences.

Indeed, what has been created are two competing systems. What may be acceptable behavior in one world may be cause for concern in the other, and vice versa. That these two worlds coexist indicates that there are two ways to become socially legitimate, and one becomes this by actively participating in one or the other of these worlds. Therefore, students who are told that they are stupid, dumb, troublemakers, lazy, incompetent, or unable in school are likely to seek social legitimacy in the real world—the world of work. Thus, many students who drop out of school tell us that they are going to work. This, apparently, is a socially acceptable answer. But it is not really an answer; it is an excuse. What they are really telling us is that they do not believe they can succeed in our world, and so they will take their chances in the world that counts. All they need to do is get a job, any job, and they have become legitimate, productive members of our society. Is it any wonder, then, that our dropout rate is as high as it is? Is it fair to blame only our nonpromoted students if they succumb to such strong temptations?

An Objection to Promotion

Today, it is clear, American education finds itself in a dilemma. In the world of education itself, we have two basic and competing value systems operating concurrently. How can we be excellent and equal at the same time? Does equality mean providing each student with similar experiences regardless of ability? If we provide different experiences in recognition of diverse ability levels, are we open to criticism about "watered-down" education? Each teacher is concerned with this objection, and one of the consequences is the question of whether to promote or not to promote. There are those who would argue in favor of retention on the basis that a student is not ready to accept the work and responsibilities of the next-higher grade. These arguments are often logical and perhaps well documented and may, in fact, be true. However, arguments and logic alone cannot suffice. It is the emotional climate and context in which the prospect of retention is presented to the student that is important. It is the fashion in which he helps influence the final decision for him that counts. Any student who intensely rejects the idea of nonpromotion in all probability should be promoted. To do otherwise might be far more damaging in the long run.

Every now and then, a researcher provides evidence to indicate that retention has beneficial effects for some students. This, of course, cannot be denied. We are not taking the position that no student should ever be retained. However, these researchers do a disservice to the profession unless they specify the exact conditions surounding the issue.

Teacher's Difficult Position as Judge

We are often asked why a student should be promoted when the teacher honestly believes he should be retained. Our answer, although simple, is not always satisfactory. We recognize, as do most teachers, that our profession is not scientific, although it is based on science. In other words, the teacher is not a scientist. It is true that we behave in concert with scientific theories of learning and theories of growth and development, but our daily behavior is not that of the scientist. In truth, much of what we do as teachers is based on folklore, intuition, "seat-of-the-pants" feelings, emotion, and educated guesses. We can never really be certain that our action in any given situation is correct. In fact, teachers are fond of saying that it takes twenty years to know how well we really did. Under these circumstances, it seems surprising that some teachers are so adamant in insisting upon retention.

The other side of this issue is that although we know about patterns of child growth and development, few if any of our students ever match the textbook version of these theories. It is possible that the student who appears to be "unready" for the next grade might well blossom forth during the summer months. More than that, he might easily become the star pupil in several years. The point to all of this is that after all these years we still do not really know. Each student must be examined individually, and the determination must be made when all the factors are considered. Perhaps it would be well for each teacher, or perhaps each school, to compile a record called "Children who surprised us." Into this record would go the case studies of students whom teachers wished to retain. Each year, some follow-up activity would take place, and the case study would be brought up to date. Thus, in time, some record would be available as a future reference. Many teachers would be amazed to learn how well some of their students do in other classes. One must always observe a certain caution, however, in utilizing this approach. Teachers should restrict their entries to the cases they honestly believe would be helped by retention; they should not load the record with the name of every student of "low ability."

Knowing the Variables

Torrance cites a number of studies that support the proposition "that different kinds of children learn best when given opportunities to learn in ways best suited to their motivations and abilities." [4] Perceptive teachers are aware that class rankings from "poor to good learners" shift position considerably with varying requirements. These position shifts evidence themselves when teaching methods change. Different kinds of mental abilities are required for different kinds of instructional materials and curriculum tasks. Likewise, the type of achievement assessment used alters the students' performance ranking; students vary in their ability to deal with timed and untimed tests, as well as essay, multiple-choice, and true-false evaluative instruments. The cognitive style of learning varies from person to person. Each child must be afforded the opportunity to follow his unique and preferred style of learning if he is to maximally achieve.

Understanding Promotion

Throughout this chapter, we have tried to say that the way the students view the situation is far more important for them than how the adults perceive it. In the issue of promotion, we would like to emphasize this point once again. The student who views nonpromotion as a threat to his personal well-being, a shock to his ego, or the spitefulness of a teacher is not likely to accept retention meekly as being in his best interests. He will build a rationale to explain why this happened. Indeed, for his own mental health, he must either develop a rationale that places the blame elsewhere or increase his negative self-reference. Under these circumstances, such a student will resent nonpromotion and begin to look elsewhere for the successful experiences he needs. Even if the teacher is correct in his assessment of the student, it will do little good for him. Perhaps it is time for us as teachers to dedicate ourselves to the purpose of helping each student. This does not mean that we work only in the academic arena; rather, our implication is that we work for the student in whatever arena he selects.

A growing body of data clearly indicates that nonpromotion (re-

[4] E. P. Torrance and R. D. Strom, *Mental Health and Achievement* (New York: John Wiley & Sons, Inc., 1965), p. 253.

tention or failure) does not favorably contribute to the educational objectives of subject-matter mastery, maintenance of standards, or pupil welfare. Policies and practices that are incompatible with continuous pupil development and growth based upon individual abilities, needs, and interests are frequently harmful. The question facing educators is not "Pass or fail?" but "What educational experiences should be provided to enhance individual learning?" In conclusion, it appears that the reasons for retention are not so compelling as to justify retention over promotion.

Summary

Since the inception of compulsory education for all American youth, teachers have been confronted with the difficult dilemma of dealing with the incompatible values of excellence and equality. Prior to the commitment of education for the masses, the dictum was simple—rigid standards of excellence for the intellectually and often financially elite. Those who were unable or unwilling to meet the standards were selected out through retention (nonpromotion or failure). Today, however, students in every state are compelled to attend school up to age sixteen. With this factor of compulsory attendance, nonpromotion must be evaluated in terms of its effect upon the clientele of the educational system.

Nonpromotion is scrutinized, in this chapter, in terms of whether it contributes to the educational objectives of subject-matter mastery, maintenance of standards, or student welfare. The evidence from various research studies demonstrates that failure does not produce the desired results. The retained student has a tendency to do less well during the year after retention than he did on comparable tests the year previously. Because teachers who find classes overloaded with retained students usually focus on the median of the group, the presence of students who have failed lowers the average, and thus work standards are also lowered. Finally, the student who has been retained sometimes becomes increasingly antagonistic, with concomitant difficulty in peer-student and teacher-student relationships.

In addition to the fact that the common reasons for retention are not mitigated by retention, the impact of failure upon the student's self-concept must be appraised. It is argued that when the student views nonpromotion as a degradation and impugning of his abilities, he is likely to see himself as one who "can't" perform. The reinforcement of this self-concept does not promise improvement. Rather, it can be expected to create new problems.

Selected Readings

Arthur, G., "A Study of the Achievement of Sixty Grade 1 Repeaters as Compared with That of Non-Repeaters of the Same Mental Age," *Journal of Experimental Education,* 5 (1936), 203–5.

Coffield, W. H., and P. Blommers, "Effect of Nonpromotion on Educational Achievement in the Elementary School," *Journal of Educational Psychology,* 47 (1956), 235–50.

Cook, W. W., *Grouping and Promotion in Elementary Schools.* Minneapolis, Minn.: University of Minnesota Press, 1941.

Goodlad, J. I., "To Promote or Not to Promote," *Childhood Education,* 30 (1954), 212–15.

————, "Research and Theory Regarding Promotion and Nonpromotion," *Elementary School Journal,* 53 (1952), 150–55.

Hall, W. F., and R. Demarest, "Effect on Achievement Scores of a Change in Promotional Policy," *Elementary School Journal,* 58 (1958), 204–7.

Otto, H. J., and E. O. Melby, "An Attempt to Evaluate the Threat of Failure as a Factor in Achievement," *Elementary School Journal,* 35 (1935), 588–96.

"Pupil Failure and Nonpromotion," *Research Bulletin of the National Education Association,* 37 (1959), 17.

Sandin, A. A., *Social and Emotional Adjustments of Regularly Promoted and Nonpromoted Pupils.* New York: Bureau of Publications, Teachers College, Columbia University, 1944.

Chapter 7

GRADING
PRACTICES

One of the major components of our educational
system, and one that seems to be inherent in most
educational systems, is the function of assigning
grades. Grading has become such a common
practice that students and parents have been conditioned to accept it as a functional dimension
of schooling. Indeed, several times each year,
teachers go through the process of evaluating
students. For many of them this amounts to
giving a series of tests, which are subsequently
scored, averaged, and entered on a report card,
which the student takes home to be signed. Unfortunately, this system is as fleeting and simple
as it is superficial and terminal, and during each

marking period teachers, students, and parents go through the same procedure. At the end of the semester, or perhaps the year, the grades are averaged and entered in the cumulative record for posterity.

Grading, however, is not an inherent dimension of an educational program. It is possible to build a program in which grades are unimportant and learning is functional. This does not mean there would be no evaluation; it does mean that evaluation would be a process rather than merely a product—which is what assigning grades is. It also means that the purposes of evaluation would be clear-cut and understandable rather than something teachers do to students. Some teachers like to tell students that the assignment of grades is similar to banking. Each test is seen as a deposit students make, and the report card is compared with a bank statement. Other teachers like to announce that they do not assign the grade, that the student himself really does that job by demonstrating his performance. No matter how teachers discuss grading, no matter what terms they use, most students view grading as a device teachers use to reward some and punish others. For all the platitudes used by teachers, grading is a force external to the student.

Grading and Self-Concept

The fact that grading students is an integral part of the present educational scene, and is sometimes viewed as a most important component, makes it a vital element in the development of the self-concept. Far too often, the grades assigned by teachers become the medium for communicating with students. In a very real sense, teachers convey their feelings as well as their opinions to students via the grading experience. While it is true that teachers provide many cues for students during the course of a working day, the payoff generally comes with the report card. The few marks a teacher places on this piece of paper often convey to the student how the teacher feels about him.

For many reasons, this procedure is most unfortunate and may be detrimental. In the first instance, the grade may be inaccurate as a description of the teacher's feelings. At best it is a rough estimate of one person's judgment. That the profession has had difficulty defining grades may say something to the teacher, and therefore the teacher may transmit an entirely different message from that which is intended. Second, students may read more into a grade than the teacher meant to imply. Assigning grades does not necessarily mean that teachers are judging anything more than performance. Certainly, this entire procedure is related to the manner in which teachers administer their responsibility. Most teachers have been exposed to the idea of differentiating between grading performance and implying a judgment in other areas. Unfortunately, we are far too successful in confusing these issues.

To the student, the grade he receives is often equated with what the teacher thinks of him as a person. Thus, a student who receives low grades believes that his teacher does not think very highly of him. Our task as teachers is to demonstrate that we can objectively review and grade performance without grading the whole person; we can hold someone in high esteem while at the same time acknowledge his weakness in a particular area. On the other hand, we must candidly admit that students get many messages from the grades teachers assign.

Purposes of Grading

Granted that in our educational system grade reports hold a central place, for what reasons do we grade? Grading is considered to be a part of the evaluative process, and therefore teachers use grades as a means of communicating with students and parents and other educators. Although this is not the only way to evaluate or communicate, it is perhaps the most common procedure used by teachers. The purpose of grading is generally conceded to be a report on a student's achievement in school and his progress in meeting educational goals. This report is generally given to parents, who are legally responsible for their children. Even more important than a report to parents, teachers have an obligation to inform the student of his progress. What we are then saying is that grading is the teacher's judgment of a student's progress toward certain educational goals and not a judgment of his development as a human being.

In addition to the major purpose of grading as stated, other purposes have evolved over time. There can be no denying that for some teachers and for many students grading is viewed as an external motivational force. Whether or not this is by design is irrelevant; grades do motivate some students. This becomes a most important factor when we realize that the results can have both positive and negative effects. For some students, high grades on a report card can spur them on toward greater effort and achievement. The student who has a backlog of successful experiences in school may be moved to improve his performance. On the other hand, low marks tell some students they are dumb, and thus can have devastating results. The student who is not doing as well as he would like to and who cannot possibly do any better will not be moved to try harder. Instead, he will probably try to find a way of rationalizing his grade. A continued succession of low marks can serve to condition a student into believing he is dull in that subject. In other words, they help him develop a negative reference of self. The real problem here is that performance in school subjects may not adequately reflect ability. The subjects themselves may be somewhat unrealistic and meaningless to a student. We recall Corey's "Poor Scholar's Soliloquy" about a seventh grader discussing his failure to do seventh-grade work. In his reactions to science, he says:

> It's funny how the Diesel works. I started to tell my teacher about it last Wednesday in Science class when the pump we were using to make a vacuum in a bell jar got hot, but she didn't see what a diesel had to do with our experiment on air pressure, so I just kept still. The kids seemed interested, though. I took four of them around to my uncle's garage after school and we saw the mechanic, Gus, tear down a big Diesel truck. Boy, does he know his stuff! [1]

The fact that such a student might get a low grade in science may not be very important, because it is not a real indication of what he is learning, but it may have a significant impact on his developing self-concept.

Nor can one deny that another purpose of reporting is to get parents to accept and strengthen the position of the school in relation to their child. Many parents unquestioningly accept a teacher's report as a true indication of their child's performance. Those little letters, which we place on report cards unfalteringly, become neon signs to parents. But teachers have an obligation to do more than simply report to parents. They must help parents accept and support their children regardless of academic performance, and they must recognize that some parents expect too much from their children while others expect too little. The teacher's responsibility, therefore, must go beyond marking the report card.

Still another purpose of grading is the pattern a student estab-

[1] S. Corey, "The Poor Scholar's Soliloquy," *Childhood Education*, 20 (1944), 19–20.

lishes in school. By the time a student gets to high school, his story in school can almost be told by his cumulative record. Thus, when he is in need of guidance for vocational and educational choices, his pattern of school progress should prove helpful to his counselor. Without a great deal of effort, a counselor obtains an overview of the student from these records.

It is important to note here that an examination of a student's performance in school provides a very narrow glimpse into his life. A counselor, and even teachers, must be prepared to look beyond the data; they must be willing to acknowledge that there is more to human life than school. If we are ever to help our students, we must go beyond information contained in school records. It is not unusual to find that a student's record is somewhat erratic over the years. This in itself should alert a counselor to the problem. Grades can be a useful tool in helping a student understand himself; they can also be a dangerous weapon in the hands of a poor teacher.

There is still another purpose of grading in school. A great deal of the research currently done in education relies on grades as a measure of performance. These research projects can be extremely valuable to teachers and administrators in providing them with guidelines to student performance and helping them understand the relationship between performance and some of the other critical variables present in a school situation. Grades may not justifiably be used in the research process, however, if they are detrimental to the student.

Bases of Grading

Probably no teacher grades students on the basis of a single performance. Grades are generally based on a series of tests, observations, and student projects. Therefore, the grades a student attains should be a fair picture of his abilities. There are certain factors in the grading process, however, which make it a tenuous practice.

The use of observation as a part of grading is probably at its maximum in the elementary school and minimum in the high school. Teachers listen to students read or discuss or recite. They observe students write, do arithmetical computation, and solve problems. Each observation helps teachers form an opinion about a student's abilities and weaknesses. Observation provides a unique opportunity for teachers to learn about functioning achievement, and can provide useful insights into student potential. It also allows teachers to note behavior and see the self-concept in action. This is a better and more accurate procedure than relying on self-reports. The study of self-concept is more valid when it is inferred from the observations of behavior, because behavior is a function of perception. Thus, it is possible to observe a variety of behavior over a period of time and then infer the perceptions that produced that behavior.

There are, however, some difficulties with the observational process which make it less useful than it could be. One of its greatest drawbacks is that by the time report cards are due the teacher has forgotten some of the things he has observed. Of course, it would be possible to record observations, although many teachers may find it quite a time-consuming procedure. To record something each day or week about every student requires so much work that it is virtually impossible. Yet, how vital this information is. Teachers observe a great deal more than academic performance or achievement. They have an opportunity to see participation and the socialization process, and no test is as adequate as these observations. They can observe directly the influence of self-concept on behavior and the modification of behavior as it takes place. In other words, they can literally observe, indirectly, the developing self-concept.

Another weakness of observation is that teachers rarely see students who are perfectly consistent. They observe extraordinary performance and pretty weak performance, and by report-card time these blend into "averageness." Also, observations are partly conditioned by the teacher's feelings about various students. Some students, no matter what the performance, can do no wrong; others can never do right. Unfortunately, observation reinforces a teacher's beliefs and feelings, and this could be disastrous to a student. This phenomenon of selective perception is well known, and it must be considered by the teacher.

Whatever may be said about observation as a basis for grading, tests and quizzes alone do not always yield satisfactory results. Few teachers know enough about test construction and validation procedures to prepare a good test. Rarely do teachers perform an item analysis or use the test to find weaknesses; that is, rarely do they use the test in a diagnostic sense. More often than not, tests are given in order to come up with a grade and are not checked for reliability. What is more, tests may be given under awkward conditions or when some students are not prepared, and some teachers, unfortunately, use a testing situation as a form of punishment. For all these reasons, grading is not always or often an objective analysis of students' ability, and students are aware of this.

Test Standards

There is still another and perhaps more difficult problem with grading and testing. Although tests may be widely used in schools today, the standard each teacher uses may be different. Some teachers establish goals that make sense to them and then measure each student against these goals whether they are realistic or not in terms of student capability. The fact that teachers are free to use these goals as an absolute scale on which to gauge performance means that it is impossible for any student to attain this goal; or conversely, all students can attain it, since this standard is independent of the student. That one can have such an external standard ignores the reality of the uniqueness of individuals. If the purpose were to determine how well one class performs in relation to the rest of the state or country, that is one thing. However, if the purpose of education is to provide each student with an opportunity to live and learn in many areas, an external standard makes little sense. Our task should be to help students explore many areas of endeavor so as to determine for themselves their strengths and weaknesses.

Of course, if this type of standard is going to be used, then one might argue that the standard could best be set by a specialist in the subject field. This makes more sense than allowing each teacher to establish an independent standard. The major problem with this approach, however, is that it implies that all teachers should have the same objectives. Even if it were desirable, it is virtually impossible to get teachers to agree on common objectives. To do so, of course, would deny any recognition of the differences among students in terms of abilities and interests.

Another standard commonly used is to establish the group performance of students as the standard. Popularly referred to as "grading on the curve," this procedure means that the criterion is dependent on student performance rather than being independent of the student. While this approach appears to make sense logically, there are hidden dangers in using it. Perhaps the greatest difficulty with grading on the curve is that no one class is large enough to be normally distributed. The normal curve, which is used for many human characteristics, is generally based on quite a large sample.

A small sample, such as one class, is ordinarily not normally distributed.

The standard that most educators feel is best, yet one that is extremely difficult to implement, is to use each pupil as his own standard. If we are to be honest when we say that one of our educational goals is to help each student develop his skills and abilities to the highest level possible, then we must also be prepared to work with students on an individual level. The yardstick one uses in this situation is a determination of how well each student performs in relation to his ability. This means that teachers must know, in as positive a manner as possible, the capability of each student. It's almost like playing God—the teacher assesses the ability of the student and measures his performance against it. And yet, this is the procedure that will provide a more complete measure of effectiveness in helping students become more aware of themselves and their talents.

Using each student as his own standard is not only difficult to apply, but interpretation of the grades assigned is virtually impossible. Some teachers using this standard, it is agreed, award grades on the basis of effort rather than achievement. Since there is no external criterion, grades are assigned on how hard a student works, not on what he achieves. Some people, though, expect the grade to tell them something about a student's achievement. Using this indivdual approach, we are on dangerous ground in making such an interpretation of grades. Therefore, grades are relatively meaningless unless we know a great deal about the conditions under which the grades are assigned, the purposes of the grades, and the standards used in grading.

Where Are We?

Thus far, we have examined the function and purpose of grading with reference to several specific examples. We have noted that each technique, regardless of its merits, is fraught with danger. Each has its supporters and its critics and each is used to some extent in the grading process. The truth of the matter is that few teachers use any one of these techniques exclusively. In all probability, teachers use a combination of these procedures in assigning a grade. More important perhaps is the recognition that a grade is nothing more than a person's subjective judgment. What is important is how these judgments affect students and influence their development. Teachers must be constantly alert to their influences on the development of students and their self-concept. A teacher who uses tests or grades as a form of punishment is telling the student something about himself. Unfortunately, this does the student little good, because other people will take the teacher's grading of the student's work to indicate a somewhat reliable measure of achievement. This means that students may have great difficulty in proving that the grade is an inaccurate assessment. The real danger occurs when students internalize the grade and believe that they are inadequate beings because a teacher says so.

Teachers have an obligation to be completely honest in their appraisal of student performance, but they are also obligated to be realistic. Persons new to the profession usually overestimate the capacity of students, perhaps because they themselves have just graduated from college and their expectations are just too great. It is therefore not surprising that many students prefer a teacher who has had some experience. On the other hand, there are those teachers who revel in the reputation of being "hard-nosed." For some strange reason, these teachers equate quality with difficulty. They apparently feel that if they are tough the student will learn more. This, of course, is not always the case. Students who are free to elect such a teacher become a select group, because many students prefer to be in another class. Of course, this process aids in the development of the self-concept. The students who elect such a class are probably more sure of themselves and their abilities. Other students, those who are less certain, find that they must rationalize their decision. The toll in the developing self-concept is extracted, and these students need more successful experiences to convince them of their talents.

Sometimes teachers find it less painful to communicate with a student through his grades. Some students have confided in us that they thought they were doing well until they got the report card. This is most unfortunate. The teacher has so many opportunities to talk with students, it is a shame that these are ignored and a piece of paper is subsituted. No teacher need fear reaction from an honest appraisal if it is coupled with a sincere desire to be of assistance. As long as we live in a society where one person must judge another, we cannot avoid the fears and concerns over grading. The most we can hope to do is alleviate the anxieties that accompany the process and help students recognize that rejection is not an integral part of the process. We can and must differentiate on the basis of ability, but this does not mean that students may not have other areas of strength.

Grading must never be made a matter of life or death, and the importance of this function is too often overemphasized by teachers. It is little wonder that students view the outcome of education to be a grade report. It almost seems that little else is important.

Most students can be helped to see themselves objectively if grades are used for diagnostic purposes. When a student attains a low grade, he is often willing to try harder. What does not seem to make any sense is the need to send this report home and thus make it public. After all, school should be a place where mistakes can be made without fear, and any new endeavor will undoubtedly entail some mistakes. If students are to be graded on everything they do, they will be less eager to try new experiences and will seek the security of grades in some subject they already know. It is not difficult to document this when we note that students, at almost every level, tend to choose those subjects in which they have already demonstrated competency and success. With the threat of grades, students are unwilling to venture into the unknown; they just won't take a chance.

If grades were used rather to help a student recognize his strengths and weaknesses, and if teachers would assist students in new endeavors, our educational system would be much improved. An example of this can probably be found in any high school in the country, but this example actually happened. In one large high school in an upper-class area, relatively few students were taking any of the art classes. When asked to explain this, they noted that they were not unusually talented in this field, yet the instructor graded them on ability. The reaction was that they could not compete with artists. What they told us privately was that they had taken an art course to get an appreciation of the subject, but they were not about to sacrifice their grade-point average against unfair competition. These students are being robbed of an opportunity for exploration and appreciation because of the overwhelming importance of grades.

The developing student needs an environment that is conducive to exploration. He needs to feel secure and at the same time he needs to experience growth. Henry says:

> Another learning problem inherent in the human condition is the fact that we must conserve culture while changing it; that we must always be (more) sure of surviving than of adapting. . . . When-

ever a new idea appears our first concern as animals must be that it does not kill us: then, and only then, can we look at it from other points of view. In general, primitive people solved this problem simply by walling their children off from new possibilities by educational methods that largely through fear, so narrowed the perceptual sphere that other than traditional ways of viewing the world became unthinkable.[2]

This is not what we want for our youth. We want the opposite. Yet, we are in danger of having the grade reports accomplish this end. But, Henry argues, schools cannot be otherwise, because: "The function of education has never been to free the mind and the spirit of man, but to bind them . . . . Schools have therefore never been places for the stimulation of young minds, they are the central conserving force of the culture."[3] Can Henry be right? Is there no way out?

Evaluation Is Facilitating

Our premise, which is evident throughout this book, is that the developing self-concept of the student can be influenced, and indeed is influenced, by what we as teachers do. All debate and fancy sayings are wasted unless they become functional in the classroom. We would therefore propose that the concept of evaluation replace our current grading practices. By this we mean that an honest attempt be undertaken to view students as individuals without reference to external standards or group pressures. We mean that allowances be made for a student to be himself, to err, to try, to fail, to grow. We would hope that he might explore his universe in the form of his curriculum without the pressure of grades. We would want him to be supported in his endeavors regardless of our opinions of his probability for success. We would encourage him to seek in areas of greatest weakness without wondering about his grades. In other words, we would hope that each student have the opportunity and challenge to find himself, to explore his areas of weakness, and to strengthen his areas of competence. Even more than this, we desire that he learn about himself and others without fear, be able to recognize and appreciate human differences, and realize that each

[2] J. Henry, *Culture Against Man* (New York: Random House, Inc., 1963), p. 284.

[3] J. Henry, *Culture Against Man*, pp. 286, 288.

person is not equally gifted or talented in all areas. We trust that through these experiences he learns to tolerate, perhaps even accept, the unique contribution each of us can make.

Evaluation rather than grading means a continuous process, and a continuing process. It means that personal and class objectives are fully understood and desirable and are not listed merely because something needs to be written. These objectives are stated in behavioral terms rather than in vague abstractions. Thus, the attainment or progress being made becomes readily observable. Furthermore, evaluation implies that from time to time the individual have an opportunity to look at himself in reference to his goals. He may do this with or without a teacher; the important thing is that he do it. If progress toward the attainment of his objectives is slow or nonexistent, an effort should be made to ascertain the reasons. Throughout the process, the student is examining himself for the very best of reasons—his own.

In this evaluation process, the teacher is a facilitator who helps the student look at himself as objectively as he can, who helps the student ask himself questions, and who guides him toward finding the answers. Through this process, the student may seek to strengthen his areas of weakness by further development of certain skills. He should also be assisted to continue in his areas of competence and reevaluate his objectives from time to time.

Conditions Favorable to Evaluation

Evaluation becomes a process of helping each pupil examine and expand his own skills. In this process, the student can determine where he is and help chart the direction he may take. It is a process of establishing current needs, immediate purposes for learning, and realistic individualized standards. Evaluation does not compare students with others who are not at all alike, but compares them in terms of their own personal capacity and development. The student participates in his own assessment based on his progress toward goals previously agreed on by both teacher and student. The question is not how many of the "right" things the student remembered, what the student did to the subject, or how well he compared with others. It is rather how well did the student do in the things the teacher and student agreed were important, what the subject did to the student, and how he compared to his own goals and objectives. Evaluation and assessment can be used to foster an accurate yet favorable self-concept. This approach need not be a downgrading of standards. Is it not possible, or even likely, that many of the standards the schools set are restrictive to learning by underestimating the student's full potential? When students help set standards for themselves, they might often exceed the ones we would have set.

There is little likelihood that the process of evaluation will replace grading unless teachers provide students with a great degree of freedom and willingness to talk about their problems and the subjects that cause them concern. In many classrooms there is little tendency for the teacher to discuss frankly those things that are not going well. In fact, the more intimately associated one is with the class program, the more reluctant one is to discuss its limitations. The reasons are varied, but most people have learned that it is safer to say nothing, or very little, and it is easier to project the responsibility for failure on someone else.

Much has been written in recent years about the importance of providing a permissive atmosphere in the classroom. The value of this psychological climate is that it enables people to express the truth, as they see it, without running the risk of being "cut down." It is only in such a climate that students can be helped to be free to examine themselves and be confident to pursue their studies. It is in this setting that the developing concept of self can be nurtured to produce a being who is more capable of finding his place in the world than if he were merely given grades. And it is through this type of class that teachers can find fulfillment of the highest ideals of the profession.

Summary

The primary purpose of grading is to report on a student's achievement in school and his progress in meeting certain educational goals. Other reasons for grading, which are peripheral to the stated purpose, are the need for external motivation, parental support of the teacher's position, the cumulative records needed for guidance and counseling, and information frequently used in educational research. Each of these reasons has some justification and some dangers. The teacher's judgment is often biased. External motivation can be devastating to the student who cannot possibly do better even with additional effort. Many parents accept teacher judgments of their child's performance irrespective of the child's ability. Cumulative records and research have value to the extent that they are reliable indicators of the student's educational pattern.

The bases for determining grades are usually tests, observations, and performance on selected projects. Observation provides a valuable appraisal of functioning achievement and the socialization process when anecdotal records are kept on a regularly scheduled basis. Nevertheless, without a systematic record of behavior and the probability of considerable teacher bias, observation has definite weaknesses. On the other hand, tests and quizzes have the potential for greater objectivity in grading. These devices are often unsatisfactory, however, when teachers lack knowledge of test construction, validation procedures, and statistical concepts. Even the use of standardized tests does not always meet the specialized needs of the classroom.

The use of preestablished standards is often based on a premise that fails to recognize that each student progresses according to his own unique pattern along with chronological age. Some children who develop late progress slowly while others progress rapidly. Expectancies and goals should be individually set—accurate, realistic, and within the capacity of each student. Goals set too high abort their intended purpose of elevation and merely disillusion and discourage. On the other hand, goals set too low create apathy and boredom.

Evaluation should be a process of helping each student examine and expand his own skills. Here, the student participates in his own assessment based on his progress toward previously agreed-on goals. In this process, the student can determine where he is and help chart the direction he may take. The question is how well did the student do in things the teacher and student agreed were important, what the subject did to the student, and how well did his effort compare to his goals and objectives. Evaluation provides a basis for current needs and establishes immediate purposes for learning.

Selected Readings

Adkins, D. C., "Principles Underlying Observational Techniques of Evaluation," *Educational and Psychological Measurement,* 11 (1951), 29–51.

Bayley, N., "Consistency and Variability in the Growth of Intelligence from Birth to Eighteen Years," *Pedagogical Seminary and Journal of Genetic Psychology,* 75 (1949), 165–96.

Black, H., *They Shall Not Pass*. New York: William Morrow and Company, Inc., 1963.

Carter, R. S., "How Invalid are Marks Assigned by Teachers?" *Journal of Educational Psychology*, 43 (1952), 218–28.

Gross, M. L., *The Brain Watchers*. New York: Random House, Inc., 1962.

Jones, H. E., "Observational Methods in the Study of Individual Development," *Journal of Consulting Psychology*, 4 (1940), 234–48.

Lorge, I., and L. Kruglos, "The Relationship Between Merit of Written Expression and Intelligence," *Journal of Educational Research*, 44 (1951), 507–19.

Michaelis, J. U., "Current Practices in Evaluation in City and School Systems," *Educational and Psychological Measurement*, 9 (1949), 15–22.

Orata, P. T., "Evaluating Evaluation," *Journal of Educational Research*, 33 (1940), 641–61.

Shane, H. G., "Recent Developments in Elementary School Evaluation," *Journal of Educational Research*, 44 (1951), 491–506.

Traxler, A. E., "Problems Arising Out of the Attempts to Apply Improved Measurement Techniques to Education and Guidance," *Journal of Educational Research*, 37 (1943), 14–18.

Wrightstone, J. W., "Trends in Evaluation," *Educational Leadership*, 8 (1950), 91–95.

Chapter **8**

CLASSROOM
DISCIPLINE

Ask any teacher what is the biggest problem in education today. The answer is bound to be that effective classroom management of student behavior is the foremost problem in our profession. Now, do not be misled by the term "classroom management." Today, this phrase is used as a synonym for discipline. For some inconceivable reason, the word "discipline" is taken to have a negative connotation, perhaps because it conjures up a picture of a teacher beating students. That connotation may be a hangover from former times. The change that has come about in the last twenty years in the connotation of the word "discipline" is not fully realized or appreciated. Hymes exhorts us to understand the term in a positive sense:

> Don't be afraid of the word. Don't be ashamed of it. "Discipline"
> is a *good* word. There is nothing old-fashioned about it. Discipline
> is as modern and as up to date as jet planes, as "miracle" drugs. One
> of your very biggest jobs as a classroom teacher is to work for disci-
> pline.[1]

Discipline Is Necessary

The need for discipline is undeniable—if we can ignore the negative connotations. In order that people may live together in a society, a set of rules and standards of conduct are demanded. Almost all our actions as individuals have an impact on other people. The more complex and complicated the society, the more interdependent and interrelated the tasks, the more we rely on others for substance and sustenance; the more we need discipline.

No team in the world of sports can be effective, regardless of the abilities of each individual, without the element of discipline. Some people like to call this "teamwork" instead of discipline. Whatever it is called, the important dimension is the ability and willingness to function within a given set of rules. It might be fruitful to examine the components of discipline in the context of a team effort. These components include coordination, commonly shared goals, arrangement of players in a particular fashion, a captain or other person designated to call signals, and attentiveness to the task at hand. In a sporting event, these components have a positive connotation and effect. In a very real sense, these same components also constitute effective discipline in the school.

It would be difficult to conceive of a class, or any other organized activity, in which these elements are lacking. The result would be chaos. Teachers cannot teach if students are inattentive. And without discipline students cannot be involved in the learnings at hand, nor can they learn without purposeful activity. No instructional program can proceed under chaotic conditions, involving interpersonal strife and reckless abandon. There needs to be some uniformity (singularity) of purpose, as well as attentiveness, coordination, and a willingness to abide by certain rules and regulations. This is what we mean by discipline. Let us emphasize here the

---

[1] J. L. Hymes, *Behavior and Misbehavior* (Englewood Cliffs, N.J.: Prentice-Hall, Inc., 1955), p. 2.

vested interest of each team member. A good performance is the commonly shared goal. A sharp contrast is drawn between team discipline and the orthodox military discipline by which each individual is subordinate to the cause. Team discipline derives from purposes and interests shared in a sporting spirit. Military discipline derives from ruling by fear and punishment.

It is important to note here that we do not subscribe to the theory that all discipline is bad. This is not to say, though, that there is no such thing as bad discipline. Basically, we view discipline as a necessary ingredient to human growth and development and a positive force in our lives. Discipline allows us to get things done, and as such it is closely related to or correlated with achievement and motivation. We would like to dispel the notion that discipline is injurious to students, and stress the value of discipline for the development of the self-concept.

Discipline Is a Part of Learning

There can be little doubt that student attitudes toward school, toward the subject matter, and toward the teacher, plus how well students learn, are influenced by the external controls exercised by those in a position of authority. In other words, the discipline used in school has a direct and influential relationship with the development of attitudes. This is not to be construed to mean that discipline is solely an external imposition on the students. Rather, we view discipline as a prerequisite to the educative process so that individual students may find adequate fulfillment in group settings.

Unfortunately, there are many educators who have chosen sides; that is, they can see no alternative to forces operating on the student from without other than to leave the student entirely on his own. To take one or other of these positions is to ignore the interaction of the corresponding external and internal forces. To fully understand the process, we must appreciate that a student, as we see him, is not a final product. Indeed, he is in a transitional state, and what we can see is nothing more than an index of his growth and development.

A danger in assuming one or other of the positions noted above consists of employing one set of techniques to the exclusion of others. Dewey provides an example of what we mean in his contrast of "old" and "new" education:

If, once more, the "old education" tended to ignore the dynamic quality, the developing force inherent in the child's present experience, and therefore to assume that direction and control were just matters of arbitrarily putting the child in a given path and compelling him to walk there, the "new education" is in danger of taking the idea of development in altogether too formal and empty a way. The child is expected to "develop" this or that fact or truth out of his own mind. He is told to think things out, or work things out for himself, without being supplied any of the environing conditions which are requisite to start and guide thought. Nothing can be developed from nothing; nothing but the crude can be developed out of the crude—and this is what surely happens when we throw the child back upon his achieved self as a finality, and invite him to spin new truths of nature or of conduct out of that. It is certainly as futile to expect a child to evolve a universe out of his own mere mind as it is for a philosopher to attempt that task. Development does not mean just getting something out of the mind. It is a development of experience and into experience that is really wanted. And this is impossible save as just that educative medium is provided which will enable the powers and interests that have been selected as valuable to function. They must operate, and how they operate will depend almost entirely upon the stimuli which surround them and the material upon which they exercise themselves. The problem of direction is thus the problem of selecting appropriate stimuli for instincts and impulses which it is desired to employ in the gaining of new experience. What new experiences are desirable, and thus what stimuli are needed, it is impossible to tell except as there is some comprehension of the development which is aimed at; except, in a word, as the adult knowledge is drawn upon as revealing the possible career open to the child.[2]

Dewey furthermore notes that these opposite positions give rise to a variety of terms which are then contrasted with one another:

"Discipline" is the watchword of those who magnify the course of study; "interest" that of those who blazon "The Child" upon their banner. The standpoint of the former is logical; that of the latter psychological. The first emphasizes the necessity of adequate training and scholarship on the part of the teacher; the latter that of need of sympathy with the child, and knowledge of his natural instincts. "Guidance and control" are the catchwords of one school; "freedom and initiative" of the other. Law is asserted here; spontaneity pro-

2 J. Dewey, *The Child and the Curriculum and The School and Society* (Chicago: University of Chicago Press, Phoenix Books, 1956), pp. 17–19.

claimed there. The old, the conservative of what has been achieved in the pain and toil of the ages, is dear to the one; the new, change, progress, wins the affection of the other. Inertness and routine, chaos and anarchism, are accusations bandied back and forth. Neglect of the sacred authority of duty is charged by one side, only to be met by counter-charges of suppression of individuality through tyrannical despotism.

Such oppositions are rarely carried to their logical conclusion. Common-sense recoils at the extreme character of these results. They are left to theorists, while common-sense vibrates back and forward in a maze of inconsistent compromise. The need of getting theory and practical common-sense into closer connection suggests a return to our original thesis: that we have here conditions which are necessarily related to each other in the educative process, since this is precisely one of interaction and adjustment.[3]

The purpose of discipline exercised from outside the student is to guide the individual in his growth from thoughtless dependence to thoughtful independence. Therefore, inner control, or self-discipline, is the long-range goal. Until this inner control is developed, however, the discipline must come from without. Students cannot and must not be wholly unguided and left completely to their own spontaneous activity in the educational setting. The educative process is a combination of activities in reference to a particular set of conditions, and education is the act of responding to these conditions and situations. The function of the teacher is to know a great deal about the needs, abilities, and interests of the student, as well as the conditions necessary to insure meaningful, responsive activity. These are, after all, the appropriately expected professional competencies of the teacher. Once this information is acquired, teachers must deploy their skills by varying the conditions and thereby providing students the opportunity to respond to different situations. In this way, through the student's own activities, he acquires the ability to learn responsively and responsibly. It is essential for the teacher, then, to know the needs, abilities, and interests of each student, as well as the conditions necessary to insure meaningful, responsive activity. Equipped with a knowledge of these key ingredients, teachers are obligated to provide and vary the conditions so that gradually the student's thinking faculties and activities produce in him an independent and continuing learner.

[3] Dewey, *The Child and the Curriculum*, p. 10.

Which Discipline to Use

One of the trends in the area of discipline has been a shift in emphasis from the days when teachers argued that to "spare the rod is to spoil the child" to an appreciation of what is now known as the guidance point of view. The most important question for teachers is how to administer discipline without doing damage to the student. Ideally, teachers would like to be provided with a series of "cookbook" techniques which would be applicable to specific types of behaviors within the classroom. Unfortunately, the dynamic interaction of human relations which are involved in the management of children cannot be reduced to simple recipes. Each situation and incident might revolve around a variety of personal and environmental dimensions. The strategic and crucial factors in one situation may not be equally or generally transferred to another situation. No single set of practices will or can be applied uniformly to any given behavior. Therefore, it is necessary that teachers know and appreciate some of the common causes of misbehavior as well as some of the possible preventive and corrective measures.

Discipline and Guidance (Direction)

Discipline is a part of the learning process. No one really expects children to learn arithmetic without the assistance and guidance of persons knowledgeable in the subject and skillful in the techniques of teaching. So, too, discipline is a means to an end—the internalized control of self-direction. Students may be free to explore and express themselves to the extent that they can understand the consequences of their acts. They are not, however, given the freedom to follow their desires without restraint. A. S. Neill keeps the question of freedom in perspective: "Each individual is free to do what he likes as long as he is not trespassing on the freedom of others," [4] Further, to expect an inexperienced child, with immature judgment and values, to make all major decisions and direct his behavior is simply unrealistic. Discipline is a developmental need. The three-year-old might run into the street, eat poisons, light fires, or walk into the lion's den; but he cannot *profit* from lethal mistakes. No one would

---

[4] A. S. Neill, *Summerhill: A Radical Approach to Child Rearing* (New York: Hart Publishing Co., 1960), p. 155.

suggest that we allow children to explore any of these areas at will in order to learn from them. Indeed, the consequences of action must be understood within the broad framework of knowing. This, however, does not mean that they must necessarily be experienced. Consequences of action must be understood.

The mere acceptance of or submission to authority will not foster responsible behavior; nor will obsequious compliance foster creativity or self-fulfillment. Yet, organized human society cannot function if people know no restraint nor control, if people remain unruly and unmannerly. The practical considerations of behavior contagion, class size, and the diverse student body make some rules and regulations (discipline) in the school imperative. It is not a question of whether or not to have discipline; the question is what kind of discipline. As a student progresses toward maturity, he must be given adequate time and sufficient practice at self-direction, with a corresponding release of external restraint. Thus, for our purposes, classroom discipline suggests the facilitating of techniques used by teachers in assisting students in the acquisition of self-control, orderly conduct, and purposive behavior.

Discipline Is Correction

Many forms of classroom misconduct are symptoms of how the student feels about himself as well as his needs in these situations. The student who is restive and foments disorder may be saying that school is not providing him with opportunities for successful experiences. The hostile, aggressive student who dominates or bullies other students may be indicating that he is unsure of himself and wants to feel accepted and important. The student who clowns and disrupts the class may be evidencing his need to be noticed and appreciated. On the other hand, teachers have been alerted to observe closely the student who is not a behavior problem, but who may be shy or withdrawn. By our definition, this type of student needs discipline as much as the student who is too assertive. This case needs firm guidance and warm encouragement so that he will be capable of assuming his responsibilities as a contributing member.

Students who misbehave generally have a negative self-regard. They may feel unwelcome, ugly, mean, or stupid. Often the student who misbehaves feels a combination of these self-devaluations, which may be subgrouped in the broad categories of unable and unwanted. People tend to behave in ways that are consistent with their self-concepts. Combs states: "It is the people who see themselves as unliked, unwanted, unworthy, unimportant or unable who . . . are the maladjusted: the desperate ones, against whom we must protect ourselves, or the defeated ones, who must be sheltered and protected from life." [5] Since the individual does behave in terms of the way he feels about himself, behavior change is contingent on a modification in this self-concept. Perkins suggests: "A child can succeed in gaining love and acceptance . . . and being honest and responsible only as he has incorporated these qualities and roles into his self-concept." [6] In this respect, discipline is moved out of the classification of obedience and punishment and into that of mental health.

Reasoning and Discipline

The abuses of the past led directly to a new emphasis. Instead of punishing students for all sorts of misbehaviors, real or imagined, teachers were asked to try to understand the student. They were told that in order to be able to help the student effectively, they needed to understand what made him the way he was. In order to help the student, they would need to aid him in overcoming some of the factors that blocked his way. In effect, teachers were asked to become therapists, a task for which they were poorly prepared. There is no denying that students were often used as innocent pawns at the mercy of ill-prepared teachers who assumed that their only task was to present information and that it was then up to the student to learn it. If the students did not learn the material, they were punished psychologically. If they did not behave properly in class, they were punished physically.

The new era in education brought with it a new view of discipline. Students did not need physical violence as much as they needed understanding. However, even this viewpoint was violated. Some educators and parents came to believe that all that was needed was to be understanding and sympathetic and all would be well. It was felt that reasoning with a student and helping him see why he was asked to do certain things would solve the problems of classroom misbehavior.

[5] A. W. Combs, "A Perceptual View of the Adequate Personality," *Perceiving, Behaving, Becoming* (Washington, D.C.: Association for Supervision and Curriculum Development [Yearbook], 1962), p. 52.

[6] H. V. Perkins, "Changing Perceptions of Self," *Childhood Education, 34* (1957), 2.

Neither of these positions make a great deal of sense. To discipline without understanding is to coerce a student into submission, while to understand without disciplining is to tolerate irrational behavior without meaning. Our position in this matter is somewhere between these two extremes. One needs to understand the underpinnings of the behavior, and one must also attempt to reason with the misbehaver, but it is the society through the teacher which gives meaning to action. It is in specific contexts and under certain conditions that a student learns to acquire self-control progressively.

We would like to examine some of the components that make discipline bad. In so doing, we might be able to recognize the weaknesses and hopefully avoid them.

Discipline Must Be Appropriate to Behavior

There is hardly a teacher who has not been faced with a situation where a student misbehaves. Teachers react differently to such situations, and it is not unreasonable to expect that some teachers will become so annoyed with a particular student that they will inflict punishment that may be excessive. Although it might be easy to understand why a teacher would react in such a manner, there can be no excusing it. We all get angry and annoyed at times, but it is because we are adults charged with the great responsibility that we are expected to be reasonable and prudent. No student can ever be made to understand or accept a punishment that is too severe in relation to his misbehavior. Few students expect to get away with their misbehavior, and most of them are willing to accept reasonable consequences. In fact, in some classes, students will seek opportunities to misbehave in order to belong with others in the class. They want to feel a part of the larger group. The punishment they will receive will be but a small price to pay for the psychological well-being of knowing they are a part of a larger group. This manifestation of student need should be a cue to the teacher that alterations in the group process are necessary. Students have a right to expect that the teacher will be sensitive to these needs and will not abuse his position of authority.

When a teacher behaves in an unreasonable manner, he can expect almost anything to happen. Some students will meekly submit to his will, others may do so but they will grumble about it or become obstructionistic, while still others may rebel and refuse to accommodate the teacher. How the teacher handles this situation is most important, because he may create or divert a crisis situation. We know of a teacher who, when faced with such a situation, literally backed the student into a corner. The student became furious, emotional, and irrational and did physical damage to the teacher. Although the student was duly punished, many felt that the teacher was really at fault. He had behaved in an unprofessional way and demonstrated a complete lack of responsibility. What is more, his action could be linked directly to the student's reaction.

It is not infrequent that similar events take place, and we are not willing to condemn all teachers for these actions. We have heard, however, of numerous cases in which the teacher might have avoided an ugly situation by acting in a different manner. Perhaps the real danger in these situations is that sometimes the teacher is too quick to administer disciplinary action; it would be much better if he waited until he calmed down and could view the incident more realistically. Teachers sometimes do things in anger for which they are later sorry.

Discipline Should Be Corrective

For many years, educational psychologists have debated the issue of reward versus punishment. Discipline that merely punishes a student for doing something the teacher views as being inappropriate is a dead-end street. Sheer punishment only serves to give the teacher revenge, while discipline should provide positive alternatives for action. What is more, behavior that may be inappropriate at one point in time may be desirable at another and under different circumstances. Discipline should help the student learn when his behavior is appropriate and when it is not.

It is too easy for students to make mistakes, and punishing them may lead them to believe that school is not a place for error. We know of a student who spends most of his school day reading library books. While this may appear to be a desirable condition, the math teacher becomes quite annoyed when this student comes into her class. Instead of continually telling the student that he cannot read during the math class, the teacher would do well to suggest when and where this activity would be more appropriate. In this way, the student is not simply told that his behavior is wrong, but he is also told that his behavior would be more appropriate in another setting.

In truth, many teachers establish a climate or condition in which only one type of behavior is acceptable; they provide no alternatives. It is similar to a teacher asking the class a question. Although each student in the class might offer an answer, they could all be wrong. Merely telling them they are wrong, however, does nothing to correct the situation. The fact of the matter is that there are many ways to be wrong and many ways to be right, and teachers must help students recognize the conditions under which certain answers or behaviors are wrong. This approach provides an opportunity for students to see that behavior appropriate under one set of circumstances may be inappropriate under another.

Punish the Act, Not the Person

One of our faults as teachers is that we do not often distinguish between punishing the person and punishing the act. A student who misbehaves sometimes is not necessarily thereby a "troublemaker." When a teacher begins to classify a student, it is the person rather than the act that is being punished. If a teacher admonishes a student too often about being a troublemaker, he will certainly persist in acting like one. After all, if the teacher already believes this about him, what difference does it make?

We have no easy formula for avoiding punishment of the student, but it is a critical factor in the development of the self-concept. The classification of students according to labels is self-defeating and degrading. More often than not, it is an overgeneralization: it does not provide corrective action at all, for it offers no alternatives; it is merely punishment.

We realize that the behavior called for by this approach is difficult, but the dangers of ignoring the issue are far worse. If our purpose is to offer constructive assistance, then it is incumbent on us not to do violence to a student's mental heatlh. The purpose of discipline is to provide corrective measures, not to destroy the self-image. It may be necessary for teachers to force themselves to remember that it is the act they dislike, not the student.

Discipline Is Not Education

Although we conceive of discipline as a part of the educative process, it is not in itself education. To punish a student by asking him to remain after school is one thing. To insist that he now spend his time in study is quite another. Some teachers discipline students by requiring them to do additional homework, or to write an essay, or to perform some other educational task. For the student, this action leads to the belief that homework or essay writing is punishment. Whenever he is given such a "punishment," he will wonder what he or the class has done wrong.

It is strange that teachers make a mockery of learning by allowing students to feel that education and punishment are synonymous. We have consistently been amazed to learn that a student will try out for the football team and subject himself to violent physical abuse without complaining. This same student, however, resents the outside readings and homework assignments he is given.

In attempting to ascertain the reasons for this, we have spoken to many students. In all candor, we must admit that many of them are not able to explain the difference in behavior. We have received some clues, however, that lead us to believe that the relationship of the student to the "significant adult" is of prime importance. If a student cannot perform an athletic task to the satisfaction of the coach, he may be asked to "take a couple of laps" around the field. The important thing is that the student perceives this not as punishment, but as a challenge. On the other hand, many students view class assignments and homework as something the teacher does just to keep them busy. They see little relevance or meaning in such chores. This interesting comparison provides a challenge to the classroom teacher to make education something more than telling.

If the examples given above are examples of bad discipline, then good discipline—to say the least—is the avoidance of these mistakes. Really, good discipline must be more than that. Good discipline is so interrelated with the teaching-learning act that it is difficult to separate it from this process.

In order to provide good discipline, the teacher needs to know a great deal about the student—about his interests, his abilities, his achievements, his desires, and his goals. In addition, it would be helpful to know something about his home life, his friends, his hobbies, the sports he likes, and his habits. Teachers must accept the fact that not all students will be capable of performing at grade level, and a student is not helped if he is constantly criticized for being behind the other students.

Contacts should be made early in the year with each student individually. First impressions are difficult to change, and teachers should try to make a good first impression. Above all, they should strive to be fair in dealing with the students. It would be well worth the time it takes to discover how the students perceive the teacher.

The goals we set for ourselves and our students should be realistic and attainable. This means that the goals may and should vary from student to student. It also means that a mistake can be made, and from this comes the realization that the goal set is too high or perhaps too low. When this happens, we should not hesitate to correct it. If too much is expected, the sights should be lowered without degrading the student. As each student demonstrates an ability and willingness to assume more and more responsibility for his growth, he should be given encouragement and opportunity to do so.

One important point that must be made here is that even if a teacher does all of these things, there is no guarantee that the desired behavior on the part of the student will emerge. In some cases, the student will be testing the teacher to see exactly how far he must go before he can create a tense situation. Or it may be that another teaching technique would be preferable with certain students. Perhaps it may mean that in this particular environment a certain student will not respond and should be transferred to another class. Teachers will be able to provide many more instances in which the techniques they learned do not apply. There is no easy answer to this most perplexing problem. Each teacher must select from the reservoir of methods those procedures which are most likely to be effective for him. Each must assess himself in terms of his strengths and weaknesses, his faults and foibles, his personality and character and then establish a method of working with students. We cannot transfer the effective techniques of one teacher to another unless many other factors are also present. As much as we may admire a particular teacher for the way he works with students, his techniques may not work for us. In the end, each teacher must develop his own style.

Now let's look at some of the practices which may positively influence self-concepts and thus behavior in the classroom.

Authority and Democracy

Observations of the reactions of ten-year-old boys to an authoritarian, a democratic, and a laissez-faire classroom climate were made by Lewin, Lippitt, and White.[7] Their experimental study

[7] K. Lewin, R. Lippitt, and R. K. White, "Patterns of Aggressive Behavior in Experimentally Created Social Climates," *Journal of Social Psychology,* 10 (1939), 271–99.

clearly demonstrated the superiority of democratic procedures in the development of individual responsibility, satisfying social relationships, constructive and friendly channeling of aggression, maintenance of work interests, and the ability to continue work activities in the absence of the teacher's prodding. While the democratic atmosphere might earn the disfavor of constrictive-type administrators because of the "educational noise and bustle," there was more constructive group activity, more cooperation among class members, and greater opportunity for the development of self-management by the students.

In the authoritarian climate, the boys either evidenced aggressive domination and hostility toward one another or they became apathetic, resigned, and submissive. In fact, these boys displayed forty times more overt aggressiveness toward one another when compared with the members of the democratic group. Further, the authoritarian-group members demonstrated very little interest in their school activities and work assignments. Authoritarian discipline did reduce misconduct at the outset. Over a period of time, however, there was increasing latent and active aggression. An additional cost of this technique was reduced interest in academic achievement.

The laissez-faire group was given complete freedom and maximum "permissiveness." The members in this setting displayed a great deal of insecurity and confusion. Schoolwork became secondary and little achievement in academics was accomplished. These boys exhibited silliness, aimless play, and considerable aggression.

It is an obvious matter to conclude that democratic procedures have definite advantages in classroom discipline. Dalton [8] studied the congruence between what teachers espoused as appropriate classroom control and what got translated into actual practice. The disconcerting results were that only a slight relationship existed between what teachers said they believed about democracy in the classroom and what they practiced. Most practiced a modified form of authoritarianism while claiming an acceptance of democratic principles for discipline.

Perhaps a safe speculation as to why teachers seldom in fact employ democratic practices in the classroom is that they have a fear that children will get out of hand if not dealt with strictly. This fear is probably motivated by a basic distrust of children: they're sure to go wrong if permitted to have a hand in their discipline.

[8] M. B. Dalton, "Classroom Democracy Functionally Defined and Measured" (Unpublished Ph.D. dissertation, University of Washington, 1949).

When teachers express faith in their students' desire and ability to develop self-management and to merit confidence, they will earn and deserve commendation. As we have said earlier, children are really on our side. They are seeking adequacy and fulfillment. The teacher could desire no more for his students.

In a class in which democratic discipline is established, the students help set the standards. Where children have a perception of shared objectives, a feeling of "we-ness" and cohesiveness is maintained. This cooperative action produces a common set of goals whereby each child feels that he has a stake in the ongoing process of his education and classroom behavior. A sense of belonging reduces discipline problems. When force, threat, harm, or coercion is the mode of operation, we have a restrictive style of control. Inevitably, reactions are withdrawal and submission or aggressiveness, scapegoating, and noncooperative behaviors.

Some Considerations

Some conduct problems arise from faults of the curriculum and from teacher attitudes. If the academic requirements are unrelated to the student's interests and needs and abilities, his attention will drift away from the tasks he does not understand or like. Actually, his motivations will seek out more attractive occupations such as altercations with his neighbor, noisiness, and restiveness. Activities that challenge and satisfy students will be a key to "preventive discipline."

Teachers who use harsh, punitive measures to maintain quiet, orderly classrooms produce discipline problems. As we have seen, this sets one child against another, breeds submissiveness, and often makes the teacher the target of group revolt. The dynamics of the classroom group reaches its maximum influence in a democratic climate. The teacher must be prepared to accept more activity and busy noise in this setting.

Opportunities for the discharge of built-up tensions are a necessary aspect of preventive and corrective discipline. Whether singularly or in combination, provisions for recreational activity, work itself, or "talking it out" with a confidant are recognized as stabilizing releases of tensions. Appropriate scheduling of diversionary breaks during the day for relaxation or exercise can reduce periodic behavior explosions.

Most classroom discipline can be achieved without severity and harshness. Redl and Wattenberg [9] suggest methods for behavior regulation through the reestablishment of pupil self-control and environmental modifications. A child about to lose his self-control can often be gently reminded through "signal interference" or "proximity control"; a meaningful smile or frown, a gesture, a hand on his shoulder, or teacher nearness by standing or sitting next to him. An environmental change is sometimes a valid preventive technique. Self-control can be enhanced by "situational assistance"—seating arrangement, group acceptance, provisions of appropriate child activities, instructional materials, and equipment.

Ultimately, individual responsibility, socialized behavior, and self-control spring from a person's having developed a stake in his community and good feelings about himself. This positive self-regard or worthiness grows in the fertile soil of mutual respect and kindness. Adult influence should be guided by these considerations. Acceptable behavior should be rewarded. Negative behavior that *does not infringe* on the rights of others should be ignored. Behavior that is damaging to self and others demands external control until the individual matures and can demonstrate his understanding of consequences.

Summary

The necessity of minimal external discipline as a prerequisite to internalized discipline is the content of this chapter. Team discipline in the school context is derived from shared purposes, interests, and spirit. It is here maintained that no instructional program can proceed under chaotic conditions, interpersonal strife, and reckless abandon. Until students evidence their understanding of the consequences of their behavior in the social setting, it may be necessary to impose certain rules and regulations. The purpose of discipline exercised from outside the student is to guide the individual in his growth from thoughtless dependence to thoughtful independence. Thus, inner control or self-discipline is the long-range goal.

The idea that all discipline is injurious to students is not quite true. Organized human society cannot function if people know no restraint or control, if people are unruly and unmannerly. The practical considerations of behavior contagion, class size, and the diverse student body make discipline in the school imperative. It

9 F. Redl and W. W. Wattenberg, *Mental Hygiene in Teaching* (New York: Harcourt, Brace & World, Inc., 1959).

is not a question of whether or not to have discipline, but what kind of discipline. Obsequious compliance does not foster creativity, spontaneity, or self-fulfillment. For our purposes, classroom discipline suggests the facilitating techniques used by teachers to assist students in the acquisition of self-control, orderly conduct, and purposive behavior.

Students who misbehave generally have a negative self-regard. They may feel unwelcome, ugly, mean, unsuccessful, unimportant, or stupid. People tend to behave in ways consistent with their self-concept. In a class in which democratic discipline is established, the students help set the standards. Where students have a perception of shared objectives, a feeling of "we-ness" and cohesiveness is maintained. This cooperative action produces a common set of goals whereby each student feels he has a stake in the ongoing process of his education and classroom behavior.

Selected Readings

Baruch, D., *How to Discipline Your Child*. New York: Public Affairs Pamphlet #232, 1956.

Bernard, H. W., *Mental Hygiene for Classroom Teachers*. New York: McGraw-Hill Book Company, 1961.

Brim, O. G., Jr., *Education for Child Rearing*. New York: Russell Sage Foundation, 1950.

Crow, L. D., and A. Crow, *Mental Health for Teachers*. New York: The Macmillan Company, 1963.

Discipline. Washington, D.C.: Association for Childhood Education International, 1957.

Gillman, H. L., *Helping Children Accept Themselves and Others*. New York: Bureau of Publications, Teachers College, Columbia University, 1959.

Hymes, J. L., Jr., *Understanding Your Child*. Englewood Cliffs, N.J.: Prentice-Hall, Inc., 1962.

Leonard, C. W., *Why Children Misbehave*. Chicago: Science Research Associates, Inc., 1952.

Mayer, G., and M. Hoover, *When Children Need Special Help with Emotional Problems.* New York: The Child Study Association of America, 1961.

Mohr, G. J., *When Children Face Crises.* Chicago: Science Research Associates, Inc., 1962.

Weitman, E., *Guiding Children's Social Growth.* Chicago: Science Research Associates, Inc., 1951.

Wolf, K. M., *The Controversial Problem of Discipline.* New York: The Child Study Association of America, 1953.

Chapter **9**

THE MEASUREMENT
OF SELF-CONCEPT

Many of the issues raised in this book, and some of the answers, have been based on the evidence available in the research of the profession. The study of self-concept continues to be a fertile field for researchers in psychology and education. In fact, it is somewhat surprising to note the numerous research projects that examine self-concept, measure it, determine its influence on academic achievement, and explore its relationship to other factors. These research efforts are of immense value, because they form the basis of action for the educational practitioner.

The purpose of this chapter is to take a hard look at the measurement of the self-concept; to explore some of the difficulties inherent in the measurement of the process; and to examine some of the problems one must avoid in using data from these measurements. As one reviews the studies conducted on self-concept, it becomes obvious that the methods used vary considerably, depending on research design and the factors to be measured. Brookover et al.[1] make an important point when they note that sometimes the only similarity found in the literature between one study and another is the use of the term "self-concept" in the title. In other words, many of the studies are entirely different from one another and do not at all measure the same factors. These studies do not really belong together if the only thing they hold in common is the term "self-concept."

As one reads the research literature, it becomes quite obvious that the self-concept is not an easy factor to measure. In many instances, there is little agreement on definition and great differences in theoretical orientation. Further, a close examination of the studies reveals that a bewildering array of hypotheses, research designs, and measuring instruments has been used (Wylie [2]). Under these circumstances, it is not surprising to find many different conclusions arising from the various studies. The difficulty here is for the educational practitioner to accurately assess the adequacy of the findings before attempting to implement them in the classroom.

There are understandable reasons for the difficulties that obtain in measuring the self-concept. In the first instance, attempts at research in this area have been too global; that is, they measure too many variables. Unfortunately, this broad approach makes it difficult to assess each factor independently. Another reason for some of the confusion is the fact that more often than not the researcher has developed his own instruments to test his theories. Not only are these instruments infrequently checked for validity and reliability, but they are often poorly described and almost impossible to locate. The lack of an adequate description and the difficulty in locating the instruments mean that the other researchers are denied access to them or the opportunity for replication. Therefore, one finds that many of the instruments reported in studies on self-concept have been used but once and then disregarded by other researchers.

---

1 W. B. Brookover, E. L. Erickson, and L. M. Joiner, *Self-Concept of Ability and School Achievement, III* (Cooperative Research Project #2831 [East Lansing, Mich.: Michigan State University, 1967]).

2 R. Wylie, *The Self Concept: A Critical Survey of Pertinent Research Literature* (Lincoln, Neb.: University of Nebraska Press, 1961).

Difficulties of Measurement of Self-Concept

One of the problems that obtains from the widespread interest in self-concept research is the measurement of the construct itself. While many associated problems are technological and theoretical, that is, relating to the science and theory of measurement, they affect the utility of the measuring instruments and underscore the limitations of their usefulness. Only when a measuring instrument has been tried and tested to the satisfaction of professionals in the field can it be used with any degree of confidence. If there is any value in testing and the use of other research instruments, it is in the stability of the measure and the fact that other researchers using the same instruments can observe the results under the same or varied conditions. This provides one means of verifying the conclusions drawn.

In no small part, many of the problems of measuring the self-concept are brought about by the failure of researchers to adequately define this construct. In a limited research setting, it is practical for the researcher to define the self-concept in terms of measurements on a specific test. This presents no problem, because the audience knows the definition. It is after the experiment, when the researcher seeks to relate his findings to those of other researchers, when he attempts to generalize his findings in terms of real-life situations, that the problem begins. Because of the limitations of the research setting and the narrow interpretation of self-concept needed for the conduct of the experiment, the researcher cannot logically relate his findings to the real world. When nothing more than an operational definition is given, the limits of the variable are incapable of being defined, and there can be no basis for generalization of the results.

An examination of the various definitions of self-concept will reveal that there is limited agreement among those using this term, and the definitions given are usually vague and abstract. Furthermore, many people who use this term neglect to relate it to a total theory and avoid defining it in relation to other variables. Therefore, a person reading an article that uses this term may have an interpretation that differs from what the author intended. While there may be some necessity to have an abstract definition at the beginning of an experiment, the move toward stating the outcome in terms of specific behavior is all too often a private process. What must be done in order to ensure precision in communication is that the researcher define the parameters of the variable and relate it to a total theory of behavior. When this is done, the researcher will be in a better position to compare his results with those of other researchers, and he will be better able to generalize his findings.

Absence of External Criteria

The problem encountered in working with self-concept is different from other experiments in psychology. Wylie [3] notes that the typical pattern of these experiments is to provide the subject with a stimulus whose properties are known to the experimenter and then to observe the response to this stimulus. Since the experimenter's knowledge of the stimulus is independent of that of the subject's, this provides an external criterion against which to measure the subject's response. For example, if the subject does not agree with the experimenter, then the experimenter may assume that the subject might have missed something or experienced something different from the other subjects. He might assume that the subject is withholding what he sees or perhaps does not have the verbal skills to report his perceptions accurately.

The researcher, on the other hand, does not have the advantage of an external criterion; he is interested in the stimulus as the subject views it. As such, he must infer the stimulus from the subject's response to it, and he has no way of getting agreement of others about what the subject should be experiencing under specified conditions. Combs et al. note that in order to study the self-concept, one must necessarily infer its nature from observations made of the behavior of the subject. The only class of behaviors that can be used is what the subject has to say about himself. This means that self-concept is a totally private and subjective experience. By definition, it is never observable by another person, and the most the researcher can hope for is to make somewhat accurate and approximate guesses concerning the degree to which the construct exists in an individual. Combs and his colleagues feel that a more accurate assessment can be made when a larger sample of behavior is used because: ". . . if behavior is a function of perception, it should be possible to observe behavior and infer the nature of the self-perception which produced that behavior." [4] Whatever the difficulties involved in obtaining a

[3] Wylie, *The Self Concept.*
[4] A. W. Combs, D. W. Soper, and C. C. Courson, "The Measurement of Self Concept and Self Report," *Educational and Psychological Measurement,* 23 (1963), 495.

larger sample of behavior, Combs et al. believe, as we shall see, that at least it avoids many of the errors found in the use of a self-reporting instrument. Even though obtaining a larger sample of behavior may not produce a perfect relationship to self-concept, they feel that the accuracy of the description will depend on the sensitivity and skill of the observer. Since the observer can be trained to develop these skills and sensitivities, more control is given over to the experimenter.

Social Desirability

Another real problem is related to the type of question asked a subject during the course of a study, because the freedom one has in responding to a question is a determinant of self-reported responses. If, for example, the subject is allowed to give a free, unstructured report, the researcher may be unable to classify it and relate it to a total index of self-concept. On the other hand, the subject may omit certain characteristics that other investigators have shown to be important in determining the self-concept. From the opposite position, if the subject is forced to choose from among several alternatives, it is virtually impossible to learn the extent to which the measuring instrument circumscribed the response and caused the subject to give a report that does not accurately reflect his conscious feelings.

When research is conducted in the absence of external criteria, it becomes necessary to rely wholly on the information obtained from the subject. The researcher has no method for learning why the subject responded as he did. For some subjects, answering questions honestly can be most threatening. Researchers working on self-concept recognize this fact, and the literature contains references to "defensive behavior" and "self-protective responses." Another factor the researcher has acknowledged is something called "social desirability." This is generally defined as the tendency of subjects to attribute to themselves personality traits that are deemed to be socially desirable. In addition, they tend to reject those items that are socially undesirable. It does little good for researchers to attribute self-dissatisfaction to subjects who respond in this manner. The important thing is to be able to identify those subjects who respond on the basis of social desirability. Unfortunately, researchers cannot learn this with present methods.

Some researchers believe that the social-desirability factor has no effect on the results, because what a subject says about himself is a valid indication of how he feels about himself at the time he is giving his responses. While few researchers have attempted to measure the social-desirability factor, it is legitimate to assume that this factor operates in many tests of self-concept. Thus, it appears that factors other than self-evaluation influence the results obtained in using these measures.

Self-Concept Tests Are Not Equivalent

The science of testing, or psychometrics, has been improved considerably in the last two decades. The development of a test is usually subject to intense scrutiny, testing, and validation before it is offered in the academic marketplace. While no attempt will be made here to be technical, we must point out that many people who use self-concept measurements for research or practical reasons apparently assume that the various self-concept measures are interchangeable; that is, that any self-concept measure will yield the same results as any other measure. This is perhaps one of the greatest errors being made today. Although the various self-concept measures may indeed be equivalent, the researcher is obligated to provide this evidence.

One of the means of evaluating a testing device is to examine its validity. Very simply, validity is defined as the ability of the test to do the job it is supposed to do. In other words, does the test measure what it is supposed to measure? There are various ways of looking at validity. One is content validity, or whether the test covers the contents of the instructional program. Another is construct validity, or the extent to which a test provides information about a meaningful characteristic. Still another type of validity is predictive validity, or how well the test results can predict future status. Perhaps the weakest kind of validity is face validity, or simply that a test looks as if it should be valid. To many users, the various measures of self-concept appear to have face validity; that is, they look like tests. It is perhaps for this reason that all measures of self-concept are seen as being quite similar. What this really amounts to is that acceptance of face validity means that a measure of self-concept is valid if it looks like a self-concept test.

The major problem in accepting face validity as the major source of evaluating an instrument is that all a person developing such a test need do is elicit self-evaluative comments from those persons taking the test. This seems to be the only requirement for acceptance of the criterion. By definition, then, all the measures of self-concept which conform to this requirement are valid, and the logical extension is made that they are also equivalent. After all, if they achieved validity in the same manner, they must also be equal to each other. Measures of self-concept cannot be taken as being equivalent measures unless they can be shown to be related to each other to a high degree. In the absence of such an empirical demonstration, the results obtained in using one instrument cannot be generalized to results obtained using another instrument.

Self-Report

There are several problems of measurement related to self-concept that cannot be overlooked, because they underscore some of the difficulties involved in interpreting the results. One of these problems is the use of a self-report. Combs et al.[5] have argued that most of the studies purporting to explore the self-concept are not studies of self-concept at all; rather, they are studies of the self-report. The fact that many studies of self-concept rely on a self-report does not provide justification for using the terms synonymously. Combs and Soper [6] defined these concepts by noting that the self-concept is how the individual sees himself, whereas the self-report is what an individual is willing to say about himself. Although the difference in terminology may appear to be minor, Combs and his colleagues argue that the concepts are entirely different and therefore cannot be used interchangeably. They say:

> The "self-concept" as it is generally defined, is the organization of all that seems to the individual to be "I" or "me." It is what an individual believes about himself; the totality of his ways of seeing himself. On the other hand, the "self-report" is a description of self reported to an outsider. It represents what the individual says he is. To be sure, what an individual says of himself will be affected by his self-concept. This relationship, however, is not a one-to-one relationship. The self-report will rarely, if ever, be identical with the self-concept. The self-report is essentially an introspection and is no more acceptable as direct evidence of causation in modern phe-

[5] Combs et al., "The Measurement of Self Concept and Self Report."
[6] A. W. Combs and D. W. Soper, "The Self, Its Derivative Terms, and Research," *Journal of Individual Psychology*, 13 (1957), 134–45.

nomenological psychology than in earlier, more traditional schools of thought.

How closely the self-report approximates the subject's "real" self-concept will presumably depend upon at least the following factors:

1. The clarity of the individual's awareness.
2. The availability of adequate symbols for expression.
3. The willingness of the individual to cooperate.
4. The social expectancy.
5. The individual's feeling of personal adequacy.
6. His feeling of freedom from threat.[7]

Parker, following this line of reasoning, states: "If these factors do, in fact, interfere with the reliability of the self-report, self-concept study with such instruments will produce questionable results." [8]

On the other hand, many researchers believe that studies of the self-concept perforce depend on a procedure in which the subject is asked to give information about himself, because the theory necessarily demands a conscious process. Generally, this process involves a verbal or written response to one of the instruments we will describe later. The utilization of such a process rests on the assumption that the response given by the subject is determined by his conscious awareness of his world. This assumption, however, is untested, and indeed it would be naïve to take for granted that a subject's response is so determined, because a subject might give a response that is influenced by other factors. For example, the response might be conditioned by the subject's intent to reveal only what he wishes to reveal. This means that a subject could say he has attitudes and perceptions which he does not really have. In other words, a subject's response may not truly reflect his feelings or perceptions. He may answer in a way that reflects what he believes is a socially acceptable answer.

Gordon notes that researchers have used several techniques of assessing the self-concept, and the debate over which procedure is better is a meaningless one. He feels that there is no point to any argument over what is a person's "real" self-concept, since we must rely on operational definitions anyway. Therefore, he argues: "Pragmatically, the validity of any approach is governed by its utility as a predictor of behavior; and cue for teacher behavior, rather than

---

[7] Combs et al., "The Measurement of Self Concept and Self Report," p. 494.

[8] J. Parker, "The Relationship of Self Report to Inferred Self Concept," *Educational and Psychological Measurement*, 26 (1966), 692.

by any artificial standard." [9] He further contends that the concern is not with "objective reality," because the question of reality is not fundamental to a person's self-concept or his attitudes.[10] He feels that truthfulness and meaningfulness are more important, and therefore, any technique must be based on the expectation that the subject will answer truthfully.

The difficulty of this position is that these limitations are real and must be given emphasis when studying self-concept. Additionally, Gordon would leave it up to the user to determine for himself whether or not the questions to be used are appropriate. He thus recognizes that the procedures need not be precise, because they are "sundials, not clocks." The point here is well taken, because it implies approximation rather than precision and, therefore, provides the user with a justification for working with "loose data." To the extent that the practitioner can make use of the techniques and instruments to improve his sensitivity to the student, his approach is most certainly justified.

These problems are realistic limitations to the measurement of the self-concept. They must be considered when one attempts such measurement, and they cannot be overlooked when one reads the literature. The absence of systematic test development in this area is due to the fact that many researchers have been interested in testing hypotheses rather than developing tests. However, if research in this important area is to be dependable, then rigorous test construction is a necessity. It is not our purpose to downgrade the importance of self-concept. On the contrary, we believe that only by understanding the problems involved in measurement can educational practitioners avoid overgeneralization and exercise caution in their interpretations.

We do not wish to take sides here in this controversy of measuring the self-concept. Our intention is to present as simply and clearly as possible some of the problems and arguments surrounding the issue. It is true that the techniques have not yet been perfected to a point where we can have perfect measurement. On the other hand, this does not mean that nothing should be done until that point is reached. The goal of having each teacher cognizant of the importance of the self-concept is a viable one. The fact that self-concept may be difficult to measure must be recognized in order to avoid errors in interpretation. At this point in time, the instruments

[9] I. J. Gordon, *Studying the Child in the School* (New York: John Wiley & Sons, Inc., 1966), p. 54.
[10] Gordon, *Studying the Child in the School.*

used to measure self-concept are the best we have available. Continued use by both practitioners and researchers will probably reveal even more weaknesses which will hopefully be remedied at some future time. For the present, however, the teacher who desires to obtain some index of self-concept must be satisfied with imperfect measurements and the limitations of the instruments.

Summary

This chapter serves as a caution to readers in general and educational practitioners specifically concerning the limitations and restrictions of the instruments used to measure self-concept. Because of the imprecise nature of the instruments, resulting scores must necessarily be interpreted in a guarded manner. The semantic problems inherent in defining the vague, elusive qualities of the global self-concept are evidenced in much of the literature reporting on studies in this area. Little has been done to find concurrence on an operational definition, or to specify the variables germane to the self-concept. Therefore, the only thing a lot of studies have in common is the term "self-concept."

Many problems arise in the area of measurement, because self-report is misconstrued as being synonymous with self-concept. For our purposes, self-concept is how a person sees or feels about himself on a series of selected variables. The self-report may or may not represent these views and feelings. The self-report may be contaminated by such factors as emotional blocks, defenses, cultural expectancies, and test-situation rapport. Unless controls for these possible contaminants are ensured, the self-report may be a totally inaccurate assessment of self-concept.

Many of the instruments that have been used in studies of self-concept have been developed by researchers without establishing the validity or reliability of the instruments. In most cases, these instruments were not used again to observe the results under similar conditions. Thus, the degree of confidence in these instruments remains questionable. Most attempts at measurement rely on introspective self-reflections which lack the advantage of an external criterion. One alternative to this method is the use of trained observers who infer the nature of an individual's self-concept by assessing a series of sample behavior. Under these conditions, greater control is given to the experimenter. However, paper-and-pencil tests, in which the subject responds to questionnaires, rating scales, adjective checklists, and inventories, are the most frequently used in determining self-concept through introspective self-reflection and subjective self-reports.

Selected Readings

Aiken, E. G., "Alternate Forms of a Semantic Differential for Measurement of Changes in Self-Description," *Psychological Reports,* 16 (1965), 177–78.

Bennett, V. C., "Development of a Self Concept Q Sort for Use With Elementary Age School Children," *Journal of School Psychology,* 3 (1964), 19–24.

Combs, A. W., D. W. Soper, and C. C. Courson, "The Measurement of Self Concept and Self Report," *Educational and Psychological Measurement,* 23 (1963), 493–500.

Engel, M., and W. J. Raine, "A Method for the Measurement of the Self-Concept of Children in the Third Grade," *Journal of Genetic Psychology,* 102 (1963), 125–37.

Merenda, P. F., and W. V. Clarke, "Self Description and Personality Measurement," *Journal of Clinical Psychology,* 21 (1965), 52–56.

Parker, J., "The Relationship of Self Report to Inferred Self Concept," *Educational and Psychological Measurement,* 26 (1966), 691–700.

Payne, D. A., "The Concurrent and Predictive Validity of an Objective Measure of Academic Self-Concept," *Educational and Psychological Measurement,* 22 (1962), 773–80.

Payne, D. A., and W. W. Farquhar, "The Dimensions of an Objective Measure of Academic Self-Concept," *Journal of Educational Psychology,* Vol. 53 (1962).

Sears, O., and V. S. Sherman, *In Pursuit of Self Esteem.* Belmont, Calif.: Wadsworth Publishing Company, Inc., 1964.

Stephenson, W., *The Study of Behavior: Q-Technique and Its Methodology.* Chicago: University of Chicago Press, 1953.

Chapter **10**

SUPPLEMENTARY CONSIDERATIONS

When all is said and done, when the research has been reviewed and the professional literature surveyed, the major task facing the practitioner is how to implement the gleanings of the best professional advice. It would be presumptuous to assume that we here are in a position to blueprint the process of introducing the essence of what we have said into the existing instructional program. The fact of the matter is that we have considered some of the dimensions of teaching in relation to the development and dynamics of the self-concept; we have not attempted to detail the action teachers should take. Nevertheless, we believe that the concepts and principles discussed have immediate application in the classroom. We further believe that teachers are the experts in determining how best to utilize these concepts and how to establish a classroom environment that will help the teacher to work effectively with students within the instructional program. Although we have made some suggestions, we should like to present in this final chapter additional considerations for teachers.

Recognizing the importance of the self-concept does not necessarily require a change in teaching style. Although some teachers may feel that they are being asked to choose between competing systems, we do not believe this to be an "either-or" situation. Teachers are not being asked to focus on either subject matter or self-concept exclusively. We are suggesting that the development of the self-concept does take place in the reality of the classroom and in the midst of whatever dynamic exists in school activities. We believe that a teacher cannot help a student develop a positive self-concept merely by telling him that he is a valuable and worthwhile individual. This development can only be accomplished through action—behavior on the part of the teacher which demonstrates trust and respect for each student.

Positive thinking and action are potent factors and they do, indeed, work, but only when they are consistent with the image one has of oneself. When this self-image is essentially positive, one's feelings of self-confidence, dignity, self-respect, and honor are enhanced and reinforced. When positive thinking and action are inconsistent with the concept of self, they cannot work, at least not until the self-image has been changed. As we stated earlier, the self-concept cannot be changed by words alone or by intellectual knowledge. For better or for worse, the self-concept is changed only by experience. Memories of past successes act to provide the self-confidence needed for the present tasks and the impetus to move forward. Perhaps this is why the cliché "Nothing succeeds like success" has, in fact, significance.

Negative Self-Concept

Just as there are principles for the development of a positive self-concept, so, too, are there general principles that cause people to develop negative self-concepts. Teachers and others who work with students should be aware of these principles in order to avoid them. For this reason, it might be well to describe briefly some of the principles that can lead to the development of a negative self-concept.

The person who has a negative self-concept can generally be described as one who lacks confidence in his abilities, who despairs because he cannot find a solution for his problems, and who believes that most of his attempts will result in failure. His expectations, in terms of his own behavior and performance, are very low, because he believes that he can do few things well. Although everybody, at some point in time, questions his worth and place in society, the person with a negative image of self often feels humiliated by his behavior, disgraced by his failures, and inferior in many situations in which he finds himself. He continually operates on the assumption that he cannot succeed, that for some reason he is doomed to failure, and consequently that he is not a worthy being.

It is important to recognize that it is not unusual to find that feelings of inadequacy and inferiority stimulate some people to work harder in order to overcome their deficiencies. In many cases, these people even excel in their work and make exceptional contributions to society. What is necessary at this juncture is to be able to distinguish between feelings of inadequacy and the personality pattern known as an inferiority complex. The inadequate person may feel impelled to work hard so as to overcome his weakness and thereby succeed. The person with an inferiority complex, on the other hand, has a pervasive, deep conviction of his inability to overcome or improve his weaknesses and limitations. The point here is that the qualities of inadequacy and inferiority do not, in and of themselves, imply that one has a negative self-concept. Perhaps the critical factor which distinguishes a person with a healthy self-concept from one with a negative self-concept is the ability to recognize and accept with understanding one's own weaknesses and strengths. The healthy person does not dilute or denigrate his strengths through preoccupation with his weaknesses.

It would be rather easy to misinterpret what has been said here, and it is important that this not be done. There is no intent to imply that a person who has negative self-references is totally devoid of positive feelings about himself or need despair of any hope. It is entirely possible that the negative feelings a person has of self are restricted to a particular skill or task or function or situation. These feelings need not be so pervasive as to cause one to believe he is a total failure. A person need only look at himself to observe certain areas he usually avoids. Some people would never deign to undertake a job requiring the use of tools such as hammer, saw, pliers, etc.

They feel so completely inept in this area that they will seek any excuse to avoid this kind of work, and would much rather get the work done than undertake to do it themselves. The fact that a person might avoid such an area does not mean that he is a total failure. His negative image is restricted to one area, and he accepts this limitation without allowing it to become totally debilitating. It must be conceded, however, that continued avoidance of this area will produce a weak spot for the rest of one's life, but that is not to say that a person has necessarily thereby a negative attitude toward other areas.

On the other hand, we must also recognize that it really is possible for a person to be totally disabled by his negative self-concept. Under these circumstances, there is relatively little one can do, because no amount of assurance, no discussion of his abilities and worth can convince him that he has a chance for success. His logic allows him to find proof for his assumptions of failure, and objective reality is no match for what he *believes* himself to be. In other words, once a person has a conviction, he finds the experiences necessary to support this conviction. Furthermore, since perception is selective, he tends to perceive only those things which support his beliefs and ignores those which are contrary to his assumptions. The more one tries to influence such a person, the more pessimistic he becomes. These exhortations, he believes, are further evidence that he is a failure in the eyes of others and thus needs to be encouraged.

The process of developing a self-concept is based on changes to be made in attitudes, beliefs, and expectations. To some extent, expectations are the most important, since most of us tend to move in the direction of what we expect to occur. Therefore, any attempt to alter expectations must also result in a change of behavior. It is at this point that past experiences are important, because they contribute to current beliefs, predispositions, and expectations. Experiences that have resulted in failure over a prolonged period of time color one's willingness to try again and lead one to expect to fail.

Developing a Healthy Self-Concept

We have commented before that a healthy self-concept is developed in the midst of reality settings rather than through mere verbalizations. This means that teachers must be keen observers of the school scene in order to know how each student is being affected.

The teacher, then, must know what to look for; he cannot be satisfied with a simple observance of a student's performance. More than that, he must know the student's goals and purposes. The teacher must recognize that behavior is more than a response to an external stimulus; it is always a creative act on the part of the student. A teacher who knows the stage of development of his students is in a better position to look for patterns of behavior rather than for individual acts. When teachers recognize that every act has a purpose, they will know that all behavior has meaning and is not random. Thus, apparently unrelated pieces of behavior and fragmentary incidents come to provide a basis for understanding behavior.

Several basic principles underlie all of what we have said, and although many of these points have been made before in other places, they might be worth mentioning again here. They are the kinds of things many of us are inclined to forget easily. We are talking about the kinds of attitudes teachers need to facilitate the development of a healthy self-concept, the kinds of attitudes that let the student know that the teacher accepts him as he is, with all his faults and foibles. The reader is certain to recognize that the points to be made do not diagram what a teacher should do; this cannot be done. What we must be satisfied with is a set of guiding principles which provide the teacher an opportunity to develop a psychological set and mode of behavior consistent with these principles. This, of course, is easier said than done, and it is still easier to discuss these issues at a distance. The teacher who works with thirty or more students hour by hour each day often finds it difficult to practice some of what he believes. It takes a conscious effort and a great deal of hard work to make teaching practice consistent with philosophical leanings.

Encouragement

One of the most critical dimensions of teaching is to provide encouragement to each student. This is not an easy thing to do, but we must convince the student that there are many things he can do even when the task seems to be quite difficult. For each of us there is a time when the task ahead appears to be impossible of completion. And yet, were we not to try, we would be certain that it could not be done, and perhaps even be satisfied with that decision. This is negative thinking which causes people to create too many categories of things they believe they cannot do. There is a great deal to be said for having tried and failed, if only to discover what cannot be done with present abilities, knowledges, and skills. This kind of experience must never be used by the teacher to punish or belittle the student. Rather, it can be constructively employed to indicate new directions and purposes for further learnings.

As teachers, we generally believe that we can encourage and help a student even if we are not experts in the field of his interest. One need only look at some of the outstanding coaches in the world of sports and note that many of them were not exceptional athletes. It is possible then to be an effective teacher without having been an exceptional student. We do not here imply that no knowledge of the subject is necessary; what we are saying is that exceptional talent is not needed. To carry this point just a bit further, we have all had experience of some teachers who were very famous people. In some cases, being famous did not improve the quality of the teaching. Thus, having exceptional talent does not necessarily guarantee that one is a good teacher.

The teacher who can create excitement on the part of the student and an eagerness to try can provide the encouragement needed by young people. The teacher who can avoid letting his own limitations become stumbling blocks for his students can help immensely by providing the type of environment in which students are not fearful of trying. The teacher who stands by as a student performs and who is a resource agent while urging him forward is doing the kind of thing many of us believe to be true teaching. Such a teacher is providing the encouragement necessary for students to try different things. This is one ingredient frequently missing from our schools.

Mistakes Are a Part of Learning

The impression gained by far too many students is that school is not a place where one is allowed to make mistakes. Even in the early elementary grades, it is not unusual for teachers to show their displeasure with students who fail to get the "right" answer. Whether intentionally or not, students begin to worry about making mistakes for fear that they will appear stupid to their teacher and classmates. Many students manifest this concern in the way they phrase a question. They may begin by apologizing for asking a "silly question, but . . ." This is the result of something classroom experiences have done to them. Why any student should worry about asking a question is something difficult to imagine. Just how many questions are unanswered and how many more are unasked is sad to contemplate.

Our schools must be places where students can safely explore many areas. Only in this fashion can the young begin to learn something about themselves, their strengths and weaknesses, interests and attitudes. As teachers, we must never forget the long, slow, hard process that is learning. Few of us learn skills readily; for most of us, it takes a lot of time, as well as practice and patience. When teachers forget to scowl and upbraid a student for not having learned, when they begin to realize how long it takes to really learn something, and when students can be free to make mistakes and even fail in the hope that they will profit from their mistakes in the long run, then we will be in a better position to assist the students who come to us. To do otherwise is to make a mockery of education and to betray the trust of the people who send their children to school.

Success Has No Substitute

Each person has a need to be successful. One cannot go through life being a failure at everything. This basic need must be recognized by teachers; and to be honest, it usually is. The reader should not construe this to mean that students must never experience failure. What we are saying is that teachers are obligated to find areas where every student can feel successful.

This does not mean that each student must be one hundred per cent successful in all his undertakings, but it does mean that he must not fail in everything he tries. The student and his academic experiences should be brought together at a level of difficulty where success is within reach. The teacher's task is to provide the environment that meets the student's readiness to learn. It is the lag between teacher expectations and student abilities which is the root of many failure-oriented self-concepts. We must not forget that academic attainment is largely learning at a point in each student's developmental progression.

We believe, in fact, that students need not be compared with their classmates, for this ignores individual growth rates. When students are compared and forced to compete, the more able are selected and the less able are discouraged. In this situation, the less able are told that school has little to offer them for which they can be rewarded.

In order to elevate human values, emphasis must be placed on the fact that all can grow.

As teachers who work with a diversity of ability levels, we must be able to provide each student with successful experiences. This does not mean that tasks should purposely be made easier to guarantee success. What we mean is that there should be many opportunities in the classroom setting for students to be successful. The standards should not be set so high that successful attainment is impossible. On the other hand, the tasks must be challenging enough and still contain the possibility of failure. In other words, there must be a challenge which gives meaning and purpose to accomplishment, with real dangers of failure possible.

It has been said elsewhere in this book that the successes of today help precondition one to attempt something tomorrow. The elation one feels at having succeeded often provides the necessary confidence for the next task. One can accept failure now and then when one knows that one has been successful before and is likely to be so again. The lack of knowledge of success, though, and the constant fear of failure may cause one to avoid any new situation.

Be Pleased with a Good Attempt

Too many teachers appear to be satisfied only with perfection and show little patience with anything less. Unfortunately, no one is so perfect that he can always do the right thing or come up with the right answer. This is even more true of students who are in the early process of becoming. As teachers, we can hinder this process by expecting the final product instead of assisting in the process. After a period of time, when we have been working at helping students develop a particular skill and we notice that they may not yet have reached the desired goal, it is our duty to be satisfied with their attempts. We must continue to offer them aid in reaching their goals, while at the same time we must instill in them the confidence to continue. This can best be done by demonstrating that we have confidence in them and in their ability to make progress in their work.

Every student has a right to expect that his work and effort will be acceptable, and he can only be encouraged to further develop his talents when he has met with some success. Even when the final product is not as satisfactory as it might be, even when it is felt that the student can do much better than he has done, even if his classmates laugh at him, the teacher must be willing to accept his sincere attempts and give him credit for having tried. We, as teachers, must force ourselves to accept the work performed at the level at which it is performed in order to help the student do better in the future. Instead of insisting that he can do much better, we must learn to reward him for what he has thus far accomplished.

Accept the Student as He Is

Educators have preached this sermon for so many years that it hardly requires to be repeated here. And yet, students have been so little accepted by teachers that we feel compelled to say it again. The process of encouragement demands that teachers accept the student as he is—with all his talents and faults, strengths and weaknesses. After all, we really have little choice in this matter. To do otherwise is to tell the student that we cannot accept him until he does as we say. To him, this means that we do not like him. If we who work closely with him do not like him as he is and cannot accept him, how can we expect him to like himself? We *must* accept him as we find him and try to help him become the kind of person he wants to be. In many cases, the person he wants to be is very similar to the person we would like him to be. When he knows that we accept him and that we have faith in his abilities, we are then in a position to have influence with him. Without this relationship, we cannot even communicate with him and are without influence. Students desperately want to be aided, assisted, and influenced by their teachers, but they do not want to be dominated by them.

Use the Class to Help

Teachers have available to them the most potent force in changing behavior—the rest of the class. Each of us has the desire to belong, and the student who is assigned to a class is no different. Whether he will admit it or not, it is most important for him to see himself as a member of the class and to feel he belongs in the group. Several kinds of behaviors come to mind as we discuss this issue. The student who seeks to gratify all his needs through getting praise and attention from the teacher is obviously missing something from the rest of his classmates. It is unnatural for a student to expect to get all his rewards from the teacher. After all, the teacher can only reward in the academic areas and not in the social areas. The fact that he seeks so much from the teacher should be a signal that something is wrong with his relationships with the rest of his classmates.

On the other hand, one sometimes finds a student who is so well accepted by his classmates that he appears to need little reward from the teacher. Although this might be seen as a healthy sign, something is wrong. Usually the class cannot provide rewards for academic achievement; this is primarily one of the teacher's functions. For many students, to be accepted by their classmates is more important, initially, than to be accepted by the teacher. Once a student feels that his classmates can accept him, he may begin to devote his attention toward academic achievement. Since most of his rewards comes from his classmates, he may ignore the teacher's emphasis on academics until he is assured of social acceptance by his classmates.

The teacher who recognizes the importance of this factor of socialization will provide classroom opportunities for each student to find acceptance by his classmates. This may be brought about in several ways. Some teachers use seating charts in a most effective manner. They move the students around periodically and place them next to other students to maximize the influence one has upon the other. Still other teachers do not hesitate to select certain students and request them to assist the teacher in making another student feel comfortable. This arrangement may cause a student to take a personal interest in the affairs of another student. How the teacher approaches the class and how he uses the class is most important in the final resolution of the problem.

Conclusion

The process of developing a self-concept has yet to be perfectly diagrammed. There are many diverse pieces of this puzzle which can be fitted into the picture. The exact functioning of each dimension can only be approximated, not blueprinted. As one looks at the total picture it can be seen that although many of the psychological processes are known, the complete cycle is, at best, an educated guess. However, there are certain factors that are known and general principles upon which one can rely. It has been our intention to discuss these principles in the specific context of the classroom.

Our educational goals and our philosophical orientation impel us to behave in a certain fashion. There are times when we are unable to implement our beliefs and values, but this does not mean that these beliefs and values are wrong. It may be that we do not have the skills needed to do this, or it is possible that the approach we use is unsuited for a particular situation. For whatever reason one might fail, one should not give up on the possibility of some day succeeding. What most of us do is to try to get a little closer to the ideal. Each attempt provides us with more information about ourselves and the impact we have on our classes. Perhaps, in time, we may be able to provide concrete evidence for our beliefs. Until then, we have an obligation to the plausibility of the self-concept theory—in the educative process—an obligation to our profession, to our students, to their parents, and to society.

INDEX